FIAT X1/9

FIAT X1/9

A collector's guide
by Phil Ward

MOTOR RACING PUBLICATIONS LTD
Unit 6, The Pilton Estate, 46 Pitlake, Croydon CR0 3RY, England

First published 1994
This softbound edition first published 2000

British Library Cataloguing in Publication Data
A catalogue record card for this book is available from the British Library

ISBN 1-899870-51-2

Printed in Great Britain by The Amadeus Press, Cleckheaton, West Yorkshire
Bound by MPG Books Ltd, Bodmin, Cornwall

Contents

Most of the variants on display, from 1974 1300 to 1990 Gran Finale.

Introduction

The Fiat X1/9 justifiably takes its place among the most stylish of Italian car designs and is a perpetual testimony to the brilliance of Nuccio Bertone. Really good designs have an enduring quality that remains acceptable over an extended period of time. The X1/9 is such a car, still appearing to be refreshingly modern and individual, even though it was created over 20 years ago.

Eminently collectable, the X1/9 is also a very usable and practical classic car for everyday transport. It is not necessarily a financial investment, because small cars historically fail to attract the elevated prices of the high-powered exotica. More importantly, though, the X1/9 represents at the time of writing the only affordable, economical proposition currently available for the young Italian car enthusiast looking for his first sportscar. The alternative soft-tops, like the Alfa Romeo Spider and left-hand-drive Fiat 124, are both more expensive to buy and harder to insure.

There is a strong international following for the X1/9, and the potential owner would be recommended to seek a well-cared-for example through one of the various specialist clubs. However, almost five years after the last X1/9 came off the production line, pristine low-mileage examples are still generally obtainable. The opportunity to buy a reasonably priced mini-exotic, before environmental sensibility removes all the 'fun cars' from the roads, is hard to resist.

April 1994   Phil Ward

Acknowledgements

I would like to express my appreciation to everyone who has contributed to this book, in particular so many members of the X1/9 Owners Club and the Fiat Motor Club (GB), but especially: Gerry Brown, Peter Collins, Guy Croft, David Farrar, John Gaisford, Graham Gauld, Chris and Mary Harvey, Geoff Oliver and Paul de Turris.

Martin Holmes provided the Abarth Rallye photographs and Peter Collins the Radbourne racecar. Michael Ward was responsible for additional photography and graphics. Finally, special thanks to my wife Josie, for her enthusiastic support and surprising loyalty.

P W

CHAPTER 1

Project X1/1

Background to a sportscar

To understand how and why the X1/9 sportscar was created we must first examine the various development projects being undertaken at the time either by or on behalf of Fiat, and in particular the one which would lead to the family of cars with which the X1/9 would become most closely associated – the Fiat 128 range. The latter was the product of a programme of advanced experimental research covering a period of some 25 years under the direction of Dante Giacosa, who was to be responsible for many Fiat designs over a total period of 40 years. The 128 family of cars resulted from his specific researches into front-wheel drive and transverse engine layouts, which he had been pursuing for many years. As early as 1947 he had patented a transverse, flat-four engine design, although the application was not to be realized until 1964.

The 128 was directly related to a design emanating from the '123' projects of 1958–59, which involved a series of prototypes with a variety of three and four-cylinder, horizontal and upright, front and rear-engined installations. They also provided a wide range of production and engineering options, including the 123E4, which employed a transverse front-wheel-drive installation later to be adopted for the 128.

Interestingly, another 123E4 prototype subsequently inspired the Fiat 124 range, although in this instance front-wheel drive was laid aside in favour of the traditional rear axle. Apart from the Italian home market, the 124 was intended to be sold elsewhere in countries where it was to be manufactured under licence; rear-wheel drive was chosen in order to minimize the set-up costs at these foreign facilities, which was to prove a farsighted decision since the 124 is still in production in the Nineties in Russia, Turkey and India.

However, it was not until 1964 that the front-wheel-drive 123E4 prototype became a production reality, Fiat deciding that their first transverse-engined car should be sold through the Autobianchi network and called the Primula. This car was powered by the old pushrod 1,221cc (type 103) unit inherited from the Fiat 1100/1200 family.

The Autobianchi Primula was the inspiration for the transverse-engine revolution from which many cars are descended, including the 128 and X1/9. Quite clearly, the British Motor Corporation, having already established the front-drive concept with the Mini, were inspired to produce the Austin 1100/1300 and, later, the Maxi, all of which share technical and physical similarities with the Autobianchi.

To launch the Primula under the Autobianchi name indicates some nervousness by Fiat to commit themselves fully to this radical new technology. However, using the Autobianchi name enabled them to 'test the water' whilst ensuring that a possible failure of the model would not be to the detriment of the Fiat name, Fiat being sensitive to the prejudices toward non-conformist designs which at that time prevailed over technical and practical reason. They were doubtless aware of the massive retooling costs necessary for the manufacture of a radical new car – and consequently the huge losses that would have resulted if it were to prove unsuccessful. Equally, should their enterprise be demonstrated under a Fiat badge and prove to be an instant success, there could have been a premature end to the production of the elderly, but still profitable Fiat 1100.

To some extent, this concern was to prove justified, as guarded public acceptance of such a revolutionary design resulted in a cool reception for the Primula on the Italian market. Elsewhere, however, the Autobianchi was more successful, and 55 per cent of production was destined to be exported, 30 per cent of it going to France alone.

128 takes shape

As a result of the technical and commercial experience gained by the Primula experiment, the development of the 128 project began in 1966, culminating in the car's launch three years later.

Giacosa's brief was to produce a car of a size comparable with that of the Fiat 1100, one which weighed approximately 700kg, had front-wheel drive from a transversely mounted engine of about 1,000cc and independent suspension with MacPherson front struts.

The original 128 project was codenamed '1001' which, after successive developments, became 'X1/1'. In *Forty years of design with Fiat*, Giacosa explains the 'X' series of codes: "This type of coding had been suggested to me, to bewilder the journalists and other inquisitive people who were nosing about after news of our new models at the test stage. Above all, we wanted to confuse people inside Fiat, including the ones on the commercial side, who wanted to know what we were up to despite stringent orders from the presidential office that this should be a matter of the strictest secrecy."

The first full-size X1/1 mock-up was made in 1967 and final approval for three versions – two-door (785kg), four-door (805kg) and two-door estate (825kg) – was given in March 1968.

A four-door car with a truncated rear end and rear-opening hatch was also built, although it was not adopted for the final 128 range, Fiat considering a hatchback design to be too radical for the late Sixties! Instead, this design was later to be used successfully by the Yugoslavian constructors, Zastava, who built the 128 under licence. After the Italian 128 ceased production in 1982, the ZCZ Yugo kept the design in production well into the Nineties.

The innocent looking Autobianchi Primula was the result of extensive development by Fiat into the use of transverse engine layouts. It was this car that became the basis for the 128 project and ultimately the X1/9 itself.

Lampredi's new engine

The original 128 prototypes used a version of the Fiat 850 engine while Aurelio Lampredi's all-new 1,100cc unit was being prepared. Incorporating every modern innovation, Lampredi's engine had an overhead camshaft directly operating the valves via tumbler tappets. Drive for the camshaft, oil pump and distributor was transmitted from the crankshaft by a toothed rubber belt. The mechanical design would not only provide a more efficient engine, but would also allow it to be manufactured using the then current production technology.

Lampredi had already made a substantial impression at Fiat by producing the belt-driven, twin-overhead-camshaft engine for the 124 Sport range. Launched in 1966, this famous engine still continues in the Nineties in much-developed form to power a variety of performance Fiat and Lancia models. He also created the V6 for the Fiat 130, a big saloon which enjoyed only limited success, and characteristics from both the 124 and the 130 units were to be found in his new 128 engine, in particular the belt-driven camshaft and ancillaries of the 124 and the cylinder head design of the 130, in which the inverted bucket tappets also carried the valve clearance shims on top to allow ease of adjustment.

Lampredi's 1,116cc engine was a brilliant design, resulting in a smooth, reliable, high-revving power unit. It was designed to allow for a bore increase to enlarge the capacity to 1,290cc and was also developed later with a longer stroke to provide 1,498cc. Following its original application in the 128, the engine was used to power the Strada/Regata and Lancia Delta ranges and more recently has been fitted to the excellent Fiat Uno.

Slanted forward at 20 degrees, the new 'over-square' 1,116cc engine had a bore and stroke of 80 x 55.5mm, and parallel-mounted valves operated by the single overhead camshaft, the fuel being supplied by a single vertical carburettor. The compression ratio was 8.8:1 and power output was claimed to be 55bhp at 6,000rpm.

The Autobianchi Primula transmission was adapted so that it incorporated a two-shaft, all-indirect, four-speed, synchromesh unit. It had a spur gear to the final-drive, mounted below and behind the gearbox. Drive was through two unequal-length driveshafts to the front wheels.

The suspension was also a significant advance for a small Fiat in employing MacPherson struts deemed necessary for front-wheel drive. Struts were also used at the rear, combined with a transverse leaf spring, and rack-and-pinion steering was to appear on a Fiat for the first time.

The front/transverse engine layout successfully combined the maximum use of interior space with the convenience of 'square' corners and flat surfaces for manufacturing ease. The short, more direct drivetrain provided increased mechanical efficiency as it meant fewer frictional losses through the transmission.

When the 128 1100 was launched in 1969, it was an immediate success and was voted 'Car of the Year' by an international panel of judges, who were suitably impressed by the new Fiat's clever use of space, its technical innovation and its combination of power and economy.

In 1969 Fiat produced a record number of new models including the 128 saloon and estate, the 130, the 2.4 Dino and the 124 Sport 1600. They were also responsible for the Autobianchi A112, A111, Primula 65c and 'S' Coupe, and along the way they also took over Lancia and gained 50 per cent of Ferrari. Yet, despite such prolific activity, one car was still absent from this impressive catalogue of models: the Fiat 128 Spider.

CHAPTER 2

Front versus mid-engined

Bertone's designer sportscar wins the argument

In any form of industry, determination and a sound marketing strategy are essential if a designer is to have his ideas accepted and translated into tangible reality. Whoever buys a design needs to consider whether it completely fulfills their requirements and if the finished product can achieve an adequate profit in the appropriate market area.

In the case of the Fiat X1/9's design origins, the motives of two major parties involved must be considered: Fiat's requirement to include a convertible sportscar in their 128 range; Nuccio Bertone's desire to promote his design and win a new contract to replace his successful, but obsolete, 850 Spider.

Fiat wanted a simple, practical, front-engined soft-top that would appeal to the budget end of the sportscar market, whereas Bertone's preference was to build a rear-engined car that was not aligned exclusively to a single model range, but stood alone so that it was a sportscar in its own right. This difference of philosophy seems to have prevailed throughout the 16 years of the X1/9's life.

Flushed with his success following the reception given to the astonishing Lamborghini Miura, Nuccio Bertone understandably wished to continue to build cars with a mid-engined configuration. After all, in the late Sixties mid-engines were fashionable, and Bertone was to prove the competence of the concept by developing it to become the ideal race/rally layout. Another masterpiece, the Lancia Stratos, demonstrated his theory by devastating the opposition in the World Rally Championships.

Unfortunately, one wing of the Fiat management regarded mid-engines as an unjustified extravagance and an indulgence by the designer. They argued that this type of car was expensive to build, heavy, and had severely restricted interior space. At least, this was their opinion as far as Bertone's reading of it was concerned.

Fiat had requested that Bertone present a design for an 850 Spider replacement. However, when the designer offered his mid-engined idea, Fiat accused him of wanting to build a poor man's Miura. In his defence, Bertone argued that the experience gained from producing the Miura was invaluable for fulfilling the manufacturer's brief, but Fiat were not convinced. They asked for two designs, one front-engined and one rear-engined. A mid-engined drawing was not requested since the manufacturer argued that the 128 floorpan was unsuitable, and they were not prepared to go to the expense of constructing a special fabrication.

Bertone complied with Fiat's request, but he also worked on and presented a third design. However, he did reserve his best work for the variant he considered to be more in tune with the spirit of the times. Demonstrating commitment to his idea, Bertone built what he called the Runabout in 1969 – a mid-engined barchetta, which he presented as a 'dream car', although it was actually a study prototype for the X1/9. The word barchetta is translated as 'little boat', which seems most appropriate because the Runabout most certainly resembled a speedboat.

This dramatic vehicle was badged not as a Fiat, but as an Autobianchi. Popularly reported as having Autobianchi A112 mechanical components, the design study actually had

These drawings illustrate the considerable thought that went into deciding how the rear of the X1/9 should be presented. The variations in front bumper design herald future updates in appearance.

a disguised 128 engine. Perhaps the coachbuilder was testing public opinion, or maybe he intended to force Fiat's hand by indicating possible interest in the project elsewhere. In any event, Bertone was soon enjoying the confusion he had helped to create.

Two-thirds of the Runabout's underbody was made up from the 850 Spider, while the rear consisted of the 128 front sub-assembly, rotated through 180 degrees. The structure was reinforced with bulkheads and a stylish rollover bar, yet despite the rigid design, the car weighed only 730kg. Its profile anticipated the eventual X1/9 shape. When viewed from an elevated perspective, the considerable difference in front and rear track was evident, the dimensions being 1,446mm and 1,285mm, respectively.

In 1970, Bertone continued his research with rear-engined, rear-wheel-drive installations using a practical vehicle called the Shake. It shared some similarities with the Runabout, but had open front and rear bodywork in the dune-buggy fashion that was popular at the time. There were at least two versions of this prototype, one having a longitudinal Simca 1200S engine and the other the new transverse Fiat 128 installation.

In the meantime, a very convenient circumstance arose for the coachbuilder, which probably influenced Fiat's decision to accept the project. The Americans were considering adopting the new ESV safety regulations, which required sportscars to have a very rigid structure, thus effectively banning all soft-top cars. Fiat regarded the US market as a premier area, so their attitude toward the mid-engined project began to change.

Clearly Fiat were under pressure from Bertone to produce the X1/9, their hesitation to do so being based on the fact that this car was intended for the cheaper end of the market. It would probably have a high production cost and, as a consequence, a high sales price – and what about profits? Nevertheless, the design was presented to Gianni Agnelli, then head of Fiat, who approved it immediately; the Fiat management had relented and were thus finally persuaded of the benefits of mid-engines.

On the one hand, Bertone's desire for a 'stand alone', designer sportscar had paid off because the new car was never considered by anyone to be a Fiat 128 Spider – it even retained its development code as a title. On the other hand, Fiat kept the car tightly within the restricted parameters of

Consideration was given to an elongated 2+2 X1/9, as witnessed in this drawing that incorporates an additional side window.

Bertone manufactured the X1/9 bodies that were later despatched to Fiat for assembly of the power unit and transmission components.

the 128 family, choosing not to exploit the design's full potential by substantially modifying the specification to increase the car's performance.

Ingegnere Montabone, then co-director of Fiat's design department, delegated an engineer named Puleo to work on the Bertone project on behalf of Fiat. Nuccio Bertone must have been more than delighted when Puleo adopted a load-bearing structure derived from his Stratos.

The resulting chassis was very rigid and compact because

of the Stratos' competition heritage, and the design would comply with the ESV regulations, although it was not capable of satisfying the original brief because it was not a soft-top. In fact, it was more sophisticated and advanced than a conventional convertible as the removable roof could be stowed away tidily.

In addition to its exotic heritage, the X1/9 was also to be influenced by political interests. Fiat were never to treat the X1/9 as a serious sportscar, regarding it as little more than a simple 128 derivative in their regimented model range structure, but the X1/9 deserved to be a performance car in its own right.

Bertone recognized the potential of the X1/9 project, but was conscious of the fact that a substantially larger engine would require structural alterations. He had planned to make a 'super' X1/9 by expanding the dimensions proportionally to accept a higher-capacity power unit, but Fiat declined to adopt this suggestion, although, as events were to prove, they were not in disagreement with the principle.

However, Bertone did actually produce his big X1/9 – in fact, a very big X1/9 – the Ferrari Rainbow. Based on the Dino 308 GT4, the Rainbow was not particularly impressive in its appearance, although it did have a novel roof retraction feature whereby the top automatically disappeared into the bodywork. However, whether this car was intended to be the enlarged X1/9 is a matter of conjecture. It definitely followed the X1/9 theme, but also illustrated that a design on one scale does not necessarily translate successfully in another dimension. It would appear that Bertone probably over-extended the mid-engined wedge design.

Further developments of the X1/9 by Bertone included the competition Abarth Rallye, of which 200 road versions were to be built to homologate the car for international rallying. Unfortunately, this promising competition project was dropped by Fiat in favour of the 131 saloon, although Bertone did at least have the consolation of constructing the new rally car. From 1976 to 1982, the 131 Abarth was an extremely effective weapon for Fiat, winning the World Championship for the manufacturer on three occasions during that period.

Bertone considered improvements and alternatives

From March 1982 Bertone took over the complete production and assembly of the X1/9 from Fiat. At that point the Fiat title was dropped and the car then became known as the Bertone X1/9.

The first and the last. The Runabout on display at Bertone's 80th anniversary exhibition in Paris accompanied by one of the very last X1/9s. There are very few pictures that show the rear of the Runabout, which is not an entirely appealing shape. Note the very wide rear track.

throughout the life of the X1/9, including a proposed 2+2. The intention was that the wheelbase should be increased from 2,202mm to 2,500mm and the track widened by 50mm. However, Fiat decided that the substantial increase in production costs of an X1/9 2+2 was approaching that of a completely new car, so the project was not adopted.

The tenuous alliance between the manufacturer and coachbuilder was unfortunate for the sportscar enthusiast for two reasons: if both parties had worked beyond the original design brief during production, a Fiat (or Bertone) badged car could have been enjoyed that was developed to its fullest potential; secondly, if both parties had pursued their separate courses, we would perhaps have been fortunate in having two different versions. Fiat might have styled their 128 Spider in-house and produced what they desired in the first place: a simple, cheap, front-engined car using standard components. This would have been an Austin-Healey Sprite replacement and could have developed into something like the Mazda RX5. Bertone, with his X1/9, could then have been free to present an adequately-powered version of his

creation, perhaps as a mini Stratos using Lancia twin-cam power.

From a manufacturing point of view, the X1/9 was not developed to a stage where other manufacturers, in particular Toyota with their MR2, might have suffered some very stiff competition. A medium-capacity, 16-valve or turbocharged X1/9 was patently the obvious route for Fiat to have followed, and in that they failed to do so, an initiative was lost.

G.31 and X1/8 projects
Assembling the pieces of the X1/9 puzzle for this book has been more difficult than might be assumed because it has been necessary to understand the sometimes conflicting motives of the different key sources of information and their recollection of events.

Even while Fiat were apparently in conflict with Bertone over the validity of the mid-engined concept, they had actually been carrying out their own research and development. The result of this parallel activity culminated in another mid-engined car, designed this time by Pininfarina.

Although Fiat seemed to be opposed to small mid-engined vehicles, ideas for cars further along the range were apparently more acceptable. It transpires that they had been working on the project since 1964, using as a basis a car now familiar to the reader, the Autobianchi Primula.

Dante Giacosa, as head of SIRA (Industrial Company for Automotive Research) explained: "In 1964, when the Autobianchi plant at Desio was starting production of the Primula, I had an idea for turning out a sports model of this auto – a two-seater coupe with the same transverse engine, but placed behind the seats and driving the rear wheels. In fact, a transverse engine for a front-wheel-drive vehicle can easily be moved back and adapted to rear-drive. The distribution of weight that results provides optimum conditions for roadholding between tyres and the road surface."

The designs for Project G.31 were completed in 1966, and Fiat built the chassis in 1967. OSI (Officina Stampaggi

The Runabout, which was presented at the Turin show in 1969 as an Autobianchi 'dream car', was described as a barchetta, or little boat, and did indeed have something of a marine appearance.

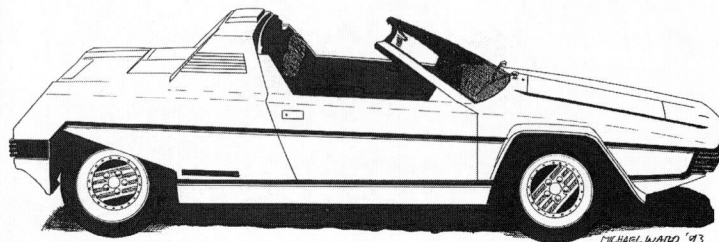

The Ferrari Rainbow styling exercise has more than a passing resemblance to the X1/9 and illustrates how the appearance of the rear-engined wedge shape changes as the proportions increase.

Industriali) built the original body. In the meantime, Giacosa was able to acquire the new Lampredi-designed Fiat 124 1,438cc twin-cam engine, and another body was designed by Pio Manzu of the Centro Stile. This delightful car had a mocked-up glassfibre body constructed in time for the 1968 Turin show – and it was displayed on the Autobianchi stand. Naturally, there was speculation that this was Autobianchi's entry into the sportscar market, but of course, the Primula engine had been replaced by the Fiat twin-cam; Autobianchi was again being used as the red herring.

According to Giacosa, the G.31 project was shelved to develop the sports models, similarly derived, using 128 components. He also claims: "The X1/9, which came out at the start of 1974, can be considered the translation into concrete terms of the concept that had led me in 1964 to design the G.31 at SIRA."

Giacosa's brief was to develop the Bertone design to accept the 128 components and running gear. His work on the engineering details included the reduction of body weight to a practical, but safe, minimum and the fitment of a front spoiler to assist the cooling airflow to the radiator.

This is not quite the end of the G.31 story, for although the project appeared to have died in 1968, another mid-engined prototype surfaced in 1970. Bertone does not seem to have been consulted for this design, the coachwork instead being entrusted to Pininfarina. The project, designated X1/8, had been set up to develop a twin-cam-powered car to succeed the Fiat 124 Sport range. In 1971, the project became known as the X1/20, and it eventually reached production in 1975. Although the car's chassis was numbered 137 in the traditional Fiat sequence, it was launched as the Lancia Montecarlo.

CHAPTER 3

X1/9's place in a growing family

Variations on the 128 theme

The 128 family was born in 1969 and the original model range arrived in the form of two and four-door saloons with the addition of a three-door estate, or Familiare. Interestingly, the Familiare was also built in Spain and South America with a five-door design.

All the early 128s were fitted with the 1,116cc engine, the 1,290cc unit eventually becoming an option that finally replaced the smaller engine, in Britain at least. The first 128s had a neat and tidy appearance enhanced by the circular headlights and chrome bumpers.

128 Rally

Although the production 128 was introduced in 1969, it was not until the spring of 1971 that any expansion of the range was implemented. The 128 Rally was the first attempt to bring a substantial power increase to the range. In one respect the Rally was the forerunner to the X1/9 because it was fitted with the new 1,290cc engine to be adopted by the forthcoming sportscar, the capacity increase being achieved by enlarging the bore diameter to 86mm; maximum power output was increased to 67bhp at 6,200rpm. However, the kerb weight of this 'sporting version' was actually heavier (820kg) than that of the 1100 two-door (785kg).

Part of the reason was that the Rally included extra equipment in the form of spotlamps and full instrumentation. Its rear light treatment was also altered, the chromium front bumper was separated and the rear quarter-windows could be opened for additional ventilation. Indeed, the Rally was to retain its chromium bumpers even when the rest of the range was updated with the straight plastic variety. However, it did forsake its circular headlamps for the oblong units which had already been applied to the rest of the range.

Beyond the 1300 upgrade, no further capacity or performance increases were forthcoming from Italy for the 128 saloon range. However, in 1982, the Sevel Fiat 128 CL Iava became available, rated at 88bhp at 6,800rpm. The only drawback was that anyone wanting to buy one had to live in Argentina! This sporty-looking car, with front spoiler and alloy road wheels, had the benefit of a larger carburettor and the later 1500 X1/9 camshaft – a useful point for would-be racing Production Saloon competitors.

128 Coupe

The 128 range was further extended by the introduction of the Sport Coupe that appeared alongside the Rally at the 1971 Turin show. Four models were presented, these being the S and SL versions with either 1,100cc or 1,300cc engines. The SL was distinguishable by its twin headlights, while the S had single rectangular units and an alternative grille treatment. The 128 Coupe became a direct replacement for the obsolete, rear-engined 850 Coupe.

The shape of the Coupe was a very successful blend of the 'house' style adopted by Fiat in the late Sixties and early Seventies, the clever design allowing a sporting appearance with accommodation for four people. Mario Boano, at Centro Stile Fiat, proved that he could produce a pleasant in-house design that followed the striking appearance of his 124 and 850 Coupe efforts. The design was so successful

The original 128 range included two and four-door saloons and the three-door Familiare. All these models were fitted with the new Lampredi-designed 1,100cc overhead-camshaft engine.

that only one prototype was considered necessary – a case of getting it right first time.

The 128 Coupe was dropped in 1974, ironically because of the enormous public interest that was being diverted to the car which was intended to complement the existing 128 range – the X1/9. Taking into consideration the circumstances where the original Fiat design brief for the 128 Spider was influenced by the coachbuilder Bertone, it is not surprising that the two models were in competition with each other: the X1/9 was proving to be too much of a coupe and not enough of a spider.

X1/9

The Bertone design for the X1/9 1300 took the form of a wedge-shaped, two-door, coupe sportscar, having a transverse mid-mounted engine located in a conventional pressed-steel monocoque structure. Retractable headlamps placed at the front corners sat above high bumpers and a prominent front spoiler.

The monocoque formed a very rigid basic structure with most of its strength in the floorpan. Box-section sills ran under the doors, with additional beam support provided by a service tunnel containing the gear linkages – the tunnel that would normally accommodate the transmission on front-engined, rear-drive cars.

A series of bulkheads supported the structure, the front one absorbing widely-spaced suspension loads and housing the radiator and pedal box. Further back, another bulkhead, situated behind the seats, supported the roof pillars and formed a built-in anti-roll bar. Two more bulkheads were incorporated, one behind the engine to support the engine/transmission and rear suspension, and the other at the extreme end of the tail.

Since subframes were not included in the design, all components were mounted directly to the body via rubber bushing. The structure was so rigid that anti-roll bars were considered to be unnecessary, which is remarkable considering the number of opening or removable panels.

The influence of Bertone continued with the interior design and layout, the driver's compartment having well-shaped seats with headrests. Space-saving ideas were implemented by placing the 10.8-gallon fuel tank behind the left seat, with the neat filler tucked away behind the left-side roof pillar. Behind the right seat was a space for the spare wheel that would traditionally have been located in the front boot. Luggage could be stowed in the front and rear compartments, the front also accommodating the removable roof panel. Access to the front and rear compartments was via handles recessed into the nearside rear wing door pillar.

The X1/9 mechanical components were sourced, predominantly, from the Fiat 128 Rally, in particular the engine, gearbox and rack-and-pinion steering. The engine unit, which had an aluminium sump, had a forward inclination of 11 degrees instead of the 20 degrees of the 128. The distributor was relocated from the original 128 position on the crankcase to the end of the camshaft. A built-in support for the accelerator linkage was mounted on the cam box, and the oil filler cap was moved to the drivebelt end.

The 128 Coupe/Rally valve timing of 24/68/64/28 and the 8.9:1 compression ratio were retained. An alteration in manifold design created a change in peak power delivery, moving it down from 6,500 to 6,000rpm. Power output remained the same at 75bhp, but the torque figure increased to 72lb.ft at 3,400rpm instead of 68lb.ft at 3,600rpm.

The 128 Rally was the first car to be fitted with the enlarged 1,300cc unit that was ultimately installed in the forthcoming X1/9. Chromium bumpers were fitted, the front bars being separated by a horizontal overrider, and additional driving lamps were provided.

A revised appearance in 1974 included rectangular headlights and a new design of bumper. At this time the 1300 engine was extended to the rest of the range.

The X1/9 1300 was 5mph faster than the 128 Coupe, although the kerb weight was 65kg (144lb) heavier than the physically larger Coupe. Gear ratios incorporated a slightly overdrive 0.96:1 top gear and a final-drive at 4.076:1. With the gearing producing 16.4mph per 1,000rpm in top gear, the theoretical maximum speed was 105mph at 6,400rpm, indicating slight under-gearing. Transmission was provided via unequal-length driveshafts of differing diameters for torsional stiffness.

The all-independent suspension system incorporated four MacPherson struts fitted with constant-rate springs. Frontal geometry was similar in layout to that of the 128. At the rear the original 128 driveshafts and hubs were mounted on large fabricated, semi-trailing lower wishbones, with an additional locating link, rotating about a semi-trailing axis. There was a high roll-centre at both ends of the chassis and the

The instrumentation on the Rally included a rev-counter. The oil pressure and water temperature gauges were inclined towards the driver.

The final evolution of the 128 saloon resulted in a cleaned-up frontal appearance created by the fitment of black bumpers with integral side/indicator lights. In 1982, the last 128s for the UK market were assembled in Ireland and are recognized by their distinctive body colours which included an appropriate emerald green. The 124-style hubcaps were replaced by plastic wheel centres.

MacPherson struts were responsible for an almost level roll axis. The front suspension lower wishbones were connected directly to the foot of the dampers, creating as a result an anti-dive effect.

The braking system consisted of hydraulic calipers on all four wheels acting on 8.95in discs sourced from the Fiat 124. The front calipers were from the Fiat 128, but the rears were similar to those fitted to the 124 range. The hydraulic circuits were split front and rear without the assistance of a servo or compensator, the basic design of the braking system preventing premature brake locking.

128 3P

The Coupe brief was reprieved and subsequently extended when, in 1975, the modernized 128 3P (tre porto – three doors) arrived. Accepting that the hatchback had become the trend, Fiat modified the 128 Coupe design to compete in the newly introduced hatchback market, the revised rear bodywork allowing the booted coupe to have a rear-opening hatch and fold-down rear seats.

As described later, in some instances the 3P was to be promoted within the Fiat dealer network in preference to the X1/9. It was the only sporty-looking small Fiat available as

Coupe styling for the 128 was successful in introducing the sporting element to what hitherto had been the range's generally mundane appearance. No fewer than four models were presented in the 128 Coupe style, two with 1,100cc engines and two with the 1,300cc units. The SL was distinguishable from the L in having twin headlights and different wheels.

an alternative to the X1/9, and not only did it have the benefit of four seats, it was actually faster, more practical and cheaper to insure than the sportscar.

With the 3P, the versatile 128 family was now complete; the range had introduced innovative technical design, which had brought benefits both to the manufacturer, through an efficient construction process, and to the motoring public, through the offer of a wide range of lively and practical vehicles. In particular, the styling of the Coupe and – even more so – the X1/9 had provided the opportunity to own striking, stylish cars that were both practical to maintain and economical to run.

It could be argued that Fiat lost sight of this area of the market when the 128 range was succeeded by the Strada. It must be said that even though the new range inherited the X1/9, it appeared to do so under sufferance, the smart sportscar effectively being ostracized by its ugly sisters and expected to fend for itself.

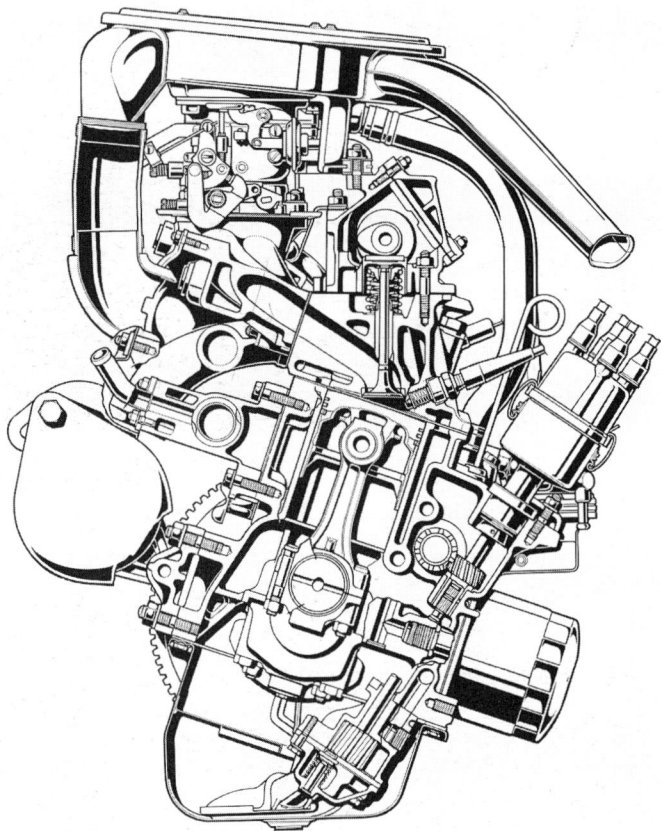

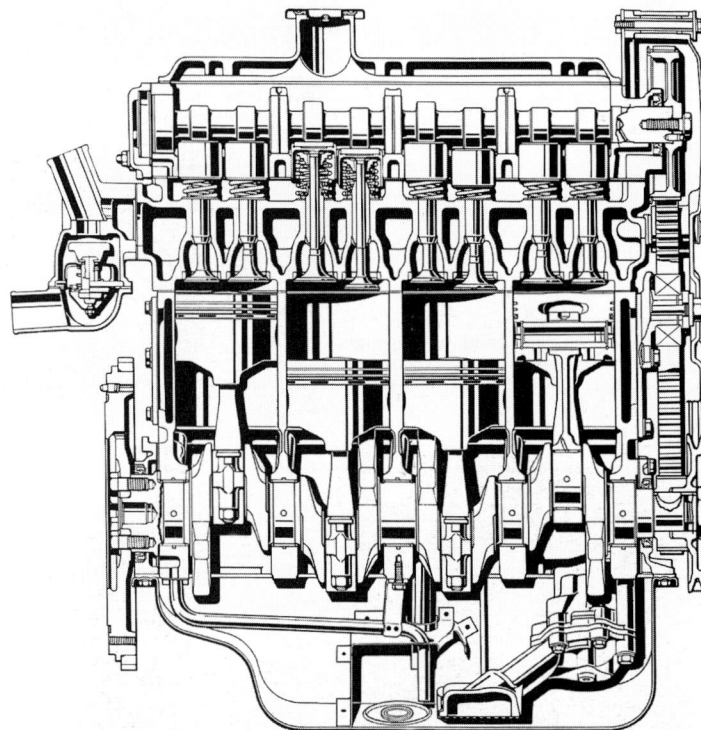

These diagrams relate to the 128 Rally engine, but that for the X1/9 is practically identical save for its aluminium sump.

Right: The revised frontal treatment thoroughly modernized the appearance of the 128, enhancing the way in which the 3P brought sporting practicality to the range.

Below right: The 3P offered a four-seater alternative to the X1/9 and eventually found itself in direct competition with the sportscar. The versatility of the 3P combined with its economy made it an attractive alternative for the sporting Fiat enthusiast with a young family and limited means.

Below: The 128 3P interior was both attractive and for the most part functional, although the tartan fabric seat inserts were not of enduring quality and soon became soiled and frayed.

However, the production history of the 128 extends beyond Italy, various models in the range having been manufactured under licence in Argentina and assembled in Colombia, Egypt, Eire, Malaysia, New Zealand, Portugal, Thailand, Uruguay and Zambia. In the main these were similar to the equivalent Italian versions, although a four-door estate was also produced in certain South American countries, while the later 3P was manufactured by the Spanish Seat company during the period when it was still a Fiat subsidiary.

This artist's impression shows how the style of the Runabout was converted into a practical production car.

CHAPTER 4

X1/9 in production

Over 160,000 cars in 17 years

With the contract secured and the design approved, Bertone commenced construction of the X1/9 bodyshells. The new car was in good company at the factory because coming off the production line at the same time were the Alfa Romeo Montreal, the Fiat Dino Coupe and the Lamborghini Uracco.

Before the X1/9 was launched, Fiat and Bertone must have had something of a fright. In an apparent attempt to steal their thunder, Alejandro DeTomaso pre-empted the X1/9 by presenting a car at the Turin show that was obviously a copy of the Bertone design. It is said that DeTomaso saw a sketch of the forthcoming Fiat and rapidly put together his own prototype.

There was some merit in the design of what was billed as the 1600 Spider-Coupe in that it had a very tidy appearance, assisted by the smooth rear engine cover; the X1/9's arrangement was arguably less pleasing. However, DeTomaso's interesting car, which was fitted with a transverse, 1.6-litre, four-cylinder Ford engine, was to prove a one-off project, but although it never went into production, it did serve as a severe test for Fiat's sense of humour.

Surprisingly, the X1/9 was launched immediately after the 1972 Turin show, and it is curious that this exotic new sportscar should have received such a low-key launch. Apparently Fiat did not wish to divert interest from another new model being presented at the show, the 132 saloon, which they regarded as a much more important commercial proposition. Although the sportscar enthusiast might argue the relevance of the 132 compared to the X1/9, Fiat were most anxious to provide a modern replacement for their 125

and considered that the 132 was the car for the job; as it happened it wasn't.

Only about 250 X1/9s were built during the remainder of 1972, and while production of the new car was being brought up to speed the outgoing 850 Spider remained under construction until the middle of 1973. At the end of that year 9,480 X1/9s had been completed, entirely for the European home market.

In 1974 the United States received their first version, and in order to meet Federal fuel emissions regulations it had to suffer a power reduction from the 73bhp of the European-standard cars to just 66bhp. A total of 20,207 X1/9s were made in 1974 for both markets, significantly over half of this production going to America, and all cars were fitted with left-hand drive.

The British motorist had to wait a further three years for an official right-hand-drive X1/9. Although Fiat SpA had offered a UK version, Fiat Auto UK decided not to import the car because their research indicated the X1/9 would be too underpowered for British tastes. The parent company accepted the suggestion of its subsidiary and reassured them that a more powerful sportscar was imminent, codenamed X1/20. Fitted with a twin-cam engine, this was to be the 124 Sport replacement. Unfortunately, the X1/20 was to suffer from both production delays and an identity crisis; Fiat's 137 chassis designation ultimately became the Lancia Montecarlo.

In the meantime, Radbourne, the prominent London-based Fiat dealers of the day, did not agree with Fiat UK's reluctance to import the X1/9 and took the opportunity to

bBERTONE

Fiat Motor Company (U.K) Ltd., Great West Road, Brentford, Middlesex TW8 9DJ

We are extremely pleased to hear that you have
recently taken delivery of a Fiat X1/9.
As you'll no doubt discover, when Bertone designed
the X1/9, great care was taken with every detail.
Particular attention was paid to an area that is
often a problem on mid-engined cars - luggage space.
We're happy to say you won't have this problem
with your X1/9, because it has been cleverly
designed with an additional luggage compartment
at the rear.
To make the most of this unusual feature,
Bertone have designed a pair of stylish soft bags
attractively trimmed to match your interior.
We have great pleasure in enclosing your set
with this letter - you'll find they fit perfectly
into the luggage space.
We're confident your X1/9 will live up to all
your expectations, and would like to take this
opportunity to wish you many miles
of enjoyable motoring.
                    yours sincerely
                    C. Shelley.
              Customer Relations Executive

A personal message from Bertone's public relations department.

convert some imported cars to right-hand drive themselves. Britain was impatient for a modern sportscar, and Radbourne realized the potential of the X1/9, having previously introduced limited numbers of the 124 and Dino Spiders to the UK market.

In 1975, a further 17,318 cars were shipped to the United States, and the first X1/9 update, the Corsa, was presented at that year's Turin show. Significantly, this car was offered not by Fiat, but by Bertone, the coachbuilder well aware that a sportier version had potential. The Corsa had special wheels, wheelarch trims and a rear deck spoiler, but retained the original mechanical specification.

During 1976, the front and rear bumpers were increased in size to suit US regulations, and at last, in October, the official right-hand-drive version was announced, although the long-awaited car did not actually appear until January 1977, by which time chassis numbers had reached the 128AS 00056000 mark. The cars which came to the UK were fitted with alloy wheels, which previously had been an option in other markets. Costing £2,298, the first right-hand-drive cars were individually numbered, had fitted luggage to match the interior trim, tinted glass, foglights, a matt-black front spoiler and a 'ladder strip' trim line. In total, 15,582 cars were produced in 1976.

During the X1/9's production life Bertone had constantly to encourage Fiat to maintain promotion of the car. Nuccio Bertone conducted his own investigation into why sales of the car had deteriorated during 1976, and he discovered that apathetic Fiat dealerships were deliberately promoting the 128 3P instead of the X1/9 – convincing potential purchasers that the X1/9 had a long waiting list and was more expensive. They were able, of course, to claim that the 3P was actually lighter, faster and cheaper, but a crucial factor was that, being an in-house design, it was probably also more profitable.

Nevertheless, Fiat agreed to relaunch the car, hence in 1977 came the next Serie Speciale. Naturally, Fiat were happy to accept the credit for the subsequent increase in sales. The special edition, introduced in the summer of 1977, was called the Lido, and from April 1978, 700 cars were made available in the UK from chassis number 128AS

The X1/9, bearing no resemblance to the rest of the 128 family, introduced an exotic flavour into the hitherto traditional range. Whereas early production prototypes had the roof panel finished in the body colour, the majority of series production cars had the panel finished in black.

Upon introduction, the Italian home market cars were fitted with steel road wheels. The original models had a chrome trim that surrounded the rear panel lighting and number-plate area.

Pop-up headlamps were a novel feature that was to cause a certain amount of grief to the owners of high-mileage cars.

The X1/9 interior was very trendy with the auxiliary switches situated on a central console, a location usually associated with more exotic and much higher-priced cars.

The purity of the first X1/9s is evident in this interior picture. Cabin accessibility had been maximized and the rear pillars were not intrusive to the occupants.

00088201. The metallic-black car sported chrome bumpers, a silver side stripe, tinted glass and white imitation suede upholstery.

The first and only power increase arrived in 1978 with the introduction of the 1500 Five Speed from chassis 128AS 00098171. The 85bhp power unit and higher-geared five-speed transmission were sourced from the new Strada range. Other changes included a new facia, luggage locker, seats and steering wheel. The engine cover was raised to accommodate the taller engine and larger air cleaner and an improved form of the '5mph' US-style bumpers were installed. At £4,575 in the UK, the new model was £500 dearer than the old 1300. Once again the unfortunate American owner received a strangled power unit, down to 67bhp, or 66bhp if living in California; in other words, the same power rating as the earlier 1300.

1978 was a good year for the X1/9 and Fiat subsequently asked Bertone to increase production, so during the

Bertone offered the first upgrade for the original car, but the X1/9 Corsa of 1975 received purely cosmetic improvement. The changes included alloy wheels fitted with large Cinturato radial tyres, wheelarch trims and a boot spoiler. The roof panel was finished in the body colour.

Fiat finally introduced a right-hand-drive X1/9 into the UK market in 1977, its smart alloy wheels becoming a distinctive feature during the years ahead. The Serie Speciale had a continuous ladder strip around the car and the front spoiler was finished in black.

Interior trimming was presented in 'deck chair' material that complemented the body colours of the car.

A youthful Niki Lauda shows off his X1/9 Serie Speciale. The numbered plaque is evident affixed to the rear of the front wing.

Serie Speciale cars were individually numbered and the badges were embellished with the national flag of the appropriate country.

following year the rate was gradually increased from 75 to 110 units per day. However, this must have happened late in the year because according to official records, the 1978 production total had been 19,240 units, and in 1979 the total output rose only slightly to 20,082 cars, this being followed by a significant drop in output to just 14,993 cars in 1980. Nevertheless, by the end of 1981, Fiat's total production of X1/9s to date had reached 140,500 cars, even though for the previous two years there had been no major styling changes or special editions to stimulate demand.

The Americans had been offered something of a power bonus in 1980 when fuel injection was offered as an option, this raising the maximum output to 75bhp. The Bosch L-Jetronic system was similar to the one fitted to the Fiat

Generations apart. An X1/9 poses next to a 1913 Tipo Zero outside PDH Motors in Brighton.

Fiat's laurel leaf badge was to remain on the front of the X1/9 until Bertone took over production in 1982.

Detail of the Serie Speciale rear pillar logo. Interestingly, the model description is recorded on the car as 'X1–9' whereas accompanying literature and consequently road test reports usually refer to the car as the 'X1/9'.

The ladder styling strip which identified the first official UK models presents an interesting challenge to owners wishing to restore the original appearance of their car.

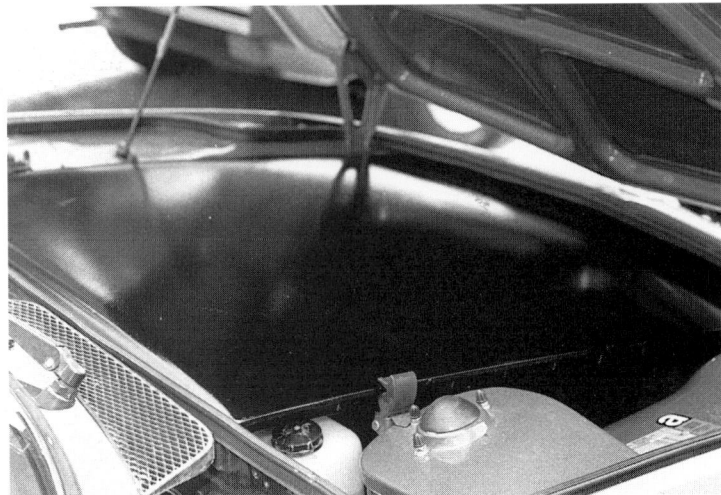

Above: Storage of the removable roof section is in the front compartment, its clever design allowing for some luggage space even when the roof has been packed away.

Above left: The external appearance of the X1/9 is very fussy in comparison with that of more modern cars; note the variety of complicated angles and shapes of these body panels.

Left: The holdalls were supplied as standard equipment and were made in the same material as used to cover the seats.

Luggage space is remarkable for such a small mid-engined car.

Spider 2000. Unfortunately, the European market did not have the opportunity to benefit from this efficient and economical installation.

Around this time, Fiat found themselves in some difficulty with their US market after reliability and quality problems led to a considerable reduction in sales. Also, the company's newer model ranges, especially the ugly Strada and the nondescript 131, won few friends. However, there was still some demand for the Spider 2000 and X1/9, so the marketing of Fiat products was assigned to IAI (International Automobile Importers), a company owned by former sportscar maker Malcolm Bricklin.

With the cessation of its own American operation in 1981, Fiat also relinquished its title to both the X1/9 and the Spider 2000. The cars were presented to the coachbuilders for their entire assembly operation, with a promise from Fiat to maintain the necessary supply of engines and other mechanical parts. At this point the models were renamed the Bertone X1/9 IN and the Pininfarina Spider Azzura, respectively. During the changeover period in 1981, some X1/9s for the Italian home market continued to be produced by Fiat while Bertone initially concentrated on satisfying the US orders. Perhaps inevitably, in view of the upheaval, this turned out to be a bad year for the X1/9, and only 4,619 cars were completed.

Once the complete assembly of the X1/9 had been handed over to Bertone it soon became obvious that Fiat had lost interest in the car. Their original intention had been for the X1/9 to be the 128 Spider, so it is not surprising that the replacement of the car should be considered at the same time as the 128 range was superseded. The last 128 was built in 1982 and the first Uno appeared in 1983. However, Fiat chose not to incorporate the orphaned X1/9 into the new range as a sports Uno, and as it was not comfortable amongst its Strada step-sisters, it was simply left instead to survive on its own.

It is interesting to speculate what might have been the X1/9's future had it been decided instead to place it within the Uno family, whilst allowing it to retain its individuality. For example, the use of the Uno Turbo engine, accepting the need for some development in order to alleviate the cooling problems inherent with a rear-engined installation, would have been an interesting development. Another, and perhaps more practical, alternative engine would have have been the new 16-valve 1500 power unit planned by Fiat.

It was early in 1982, after Bertone had taken full control of production of the car, that the model was given its new Bertone X1/9 IN title, the 'IN' meaning INjection for the United States, but translated as IN Fashion or IN Vogue for the European (injection-less) market. Two-tone colour schemes were introduced, along with leather seats, electric windows and a facsimile signed plaque by Nuccio himself.

The Bertone car arrived in the UK as the VS (Version Speciale) in July 1983 and had a different style of alloy road wheel, while in 1984 yet another type of alloy road wheel was fitted.

Having disposed of the X1/9 in 1982, Fiat, of course, did not develop the model any further, and as the coachbuilders were not best placed to implement technical developments, the model was living on borrowed time. Clearly, there was an

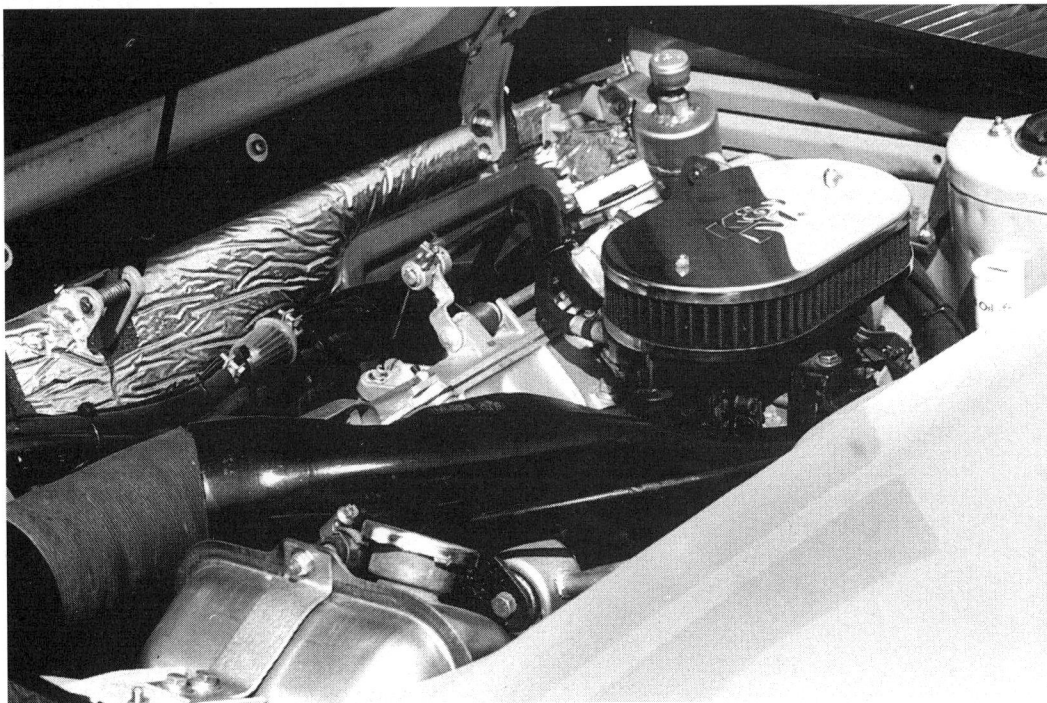

Access to the important areas of the engine for routine servicing is actually better than it might appear from this picture.

The off-white upholstery was very smart, but not entirely practical for everyday use.

Originally intended as a special edition for the Swiss market, the Lido, named after the famous Paris night club that was used for the car's launch, became available in the UK during 1978. Fiat's publicity department made extensive use of the black and white theme adopted for the car's colour scheme.

The Lido was the only X1/9 to have been fitted with chrome bumpers throughout its production life.

This immaculate Lido is a very rare, original, low-mileage and unre-stored car that at the time of writing was owned by Geoff Oliver of London's X1/9 Centre.

The paint finish on the Lido was metallic black with a fairly heavy and distinctive silver fleck.

The first and only engine capacity increase arrived with the X1/9 1500 in late 1978.

External alterations included a revised bumper arrangement and a higher engine cover. The ladder strips have disappeared, resulting in a much cleaner appearance.

The seating on the 1500 used a combination of vinyl and fabric that was both smart and serviceable. The strange gear-lever was universally unpopular and was often replaced.

The 1500 was badged as the X1/9 Five Speed, relating to the gearbox which had been inherited from the new Fiat Strada range.

opportunity for another constructor to take advantage of this neglect, and it was the Japanese manufacturer Toyota who in 1984 took the initiative and introduced their MR2. It had the 'civilization' that the X1/9 was beginning to lack – a quieter engine and various other modern refinements. The reader might be forgiven for wondering why sportscars should be quiet, but the plain fact was that the archetypical sportscar driver was becoming softer.

In February 1986 an additional, cheaper, basic X1/9 model was offered. It had a single-colour paint finish with

Fiat's PR department was never slow to promote the X1/9, and here a 1500 is being used by Lenny Bruce while touring the UK with his jazz band.

The version for the American market was offered with pressed-steel wheels of a design used on various other models in the Fiat range, notably the 131. The increase in bumper size necessary to satisfy American safety regulations did little for the car's aesthetics.

43

The pop-up headlamps give the X1/9 a somewhat 'frog-eyed' appearance.

A distinctive 1500 fitted with after-market wheels on display at the annual X1/9 Club meeting at the Nurburgring.

The US-market cars were fitted with this interim design of bumper in the late Seventies. This car has been registered in Germany.

Another US-specification car in Europe, in this instance Dutch-registered.

From 1980 the American-market X1/9s were equipped with Bosch L-Jetronic fuel injection, mainly to meet local fuel-emissions regulations. The injection helped to restore some performance to the restricted engine and went some way to improving the hot-starting difficulties inherent with the design.

In 1982 Bertone assumed total responsibility for X1/9 production and assembly. The first cars built under the new arrangement appeared to have had an identity crisis because some received Fiat logos on the rear quarter, like this one, badged X1/9 IN.

This very early Bertone-badged car features the low-line duotone colour scheme. A US-market X1/9, it carries the model description X1/9 LTD and is fitted with a type of alloy road wheel not supplied to the UK market.

In July 1983, the first Bertone X1/9s arrived in Great Britain, having lost the 'IN' part of their title on the way over from Italy. Known as the VS, Version Speciale, they carried the distinctive low-line colour scheme and Abarth-style road wheels. Arguably, this is the most attractive X1/9 specification.

The letters VS seemed to have been applied as something of an afterthought and did not blend in well with the other logos. To add to the confusion, some cars were delivered without the VS symbol at all.

Leather was used to trim the interior of the Bertone car, providing the X1/9 with an air of exclusivity that the natural material usually creates in much more expensive sportscars.

From 1984, a revised colour scheme was introduced that raised the waistline, and at the same time yet another style of road wheel was fitted. The bumpers had a bright stainless steel finish and the engine covers were black.

Appropriately registered, this X1/9 VS has undergone a thorough restoration by its owner to bring it right up to concours standard.

This leather interior is both attractive and hard-wearing.

The stowage compartment for the roof section of the X1/9 VS, which was finished in the upper body colour.

In February 1986, a slightly cheaper car was introduced on the UK market to complement the VS; it had fabric seats and a single-tone colour scheme, although the difference is scarcely noticeable in this press picture.

The two-car range was revised again in 1987, a black side moulding being added to the doors and front wings. Of course, the wheels were changed yet again! This time, the bumpers were all-black, but the engine cover was painted in the body colour.

cloth seats and door panels as an alternative to the red leather of the VS. Priced in the UK at £7,555, it cost £653 less than the VS. Then in 1987 came yet another revision, identified by new wheels and side mouldings. There was still a steady demand for the X1/9, and by the end of 1988 some 160,000 units had been made.

However, time was running out for the little sportscar, and in March 1989, as production came to an end, Fiat UK marketed the Gran Finale. This very attractive car was trimmed in colourful Alcantara upholstery, had special wheels, tinted electric windows, a rear spoiler and Mica paintwork, which was offered in a choice of either blue or red metallic colours.

Although the world's motor industry in the Nineties seems more concerned with providing true enthusiasts with the sort of pseudo sportscars that are convenient to manufacture – such as hot hatches and other so-called performance derivatives of boring mass-production models – rather than cars of real individuality such as they might prefer to own, there are signs that the genuine sportscar is far from dead, and even as this is being written plans are afoot by Fiat to reintroduce the small sportscar after 10 lost years. The intention is to develop a new Spider with a transverse and front-mounted engine to fill the gap left by the X1/9. It seems that at long last Fiat are to realize their original desire for a 128 Spider!

This VS has had the appearance of its road wheels radicaly altered by its owner. The X1/9's Cromadora light-alloy wheels were inscribed with the coachbuilder's name from 1983.

Below left: An X1/9 identification exercise, which is assisted by the appearance of the bumpers, always assuming, of course, that these cars, seen at an X1/9 Club gathering, have not been altered by their owners!

Below: Access to the spare wheel is behind the right-hand seat. Some taller than average drivers have found a way of increasing the restricted legroom; if the spare wheel is relocated to the front luggage compartment and the seat belt anchorage resited, additional rear movement is achieved for the seat.

The Gran Finale brought to a close the production of this great little car in March 1989. Although the bodyshell had remained unchanged throughout its production, progressive revision of the trim and paint finishes were used to update the car from time to time and maintain its acceptance in the market for small sportscars.

The identifying script of the last cars replaced the original rear wing vent.

The appearance of the car was brought up-to-date mainly through the choice of metallic paint finishes and expensive-looking road wheels.

A bright stainless-steel finish was re-introduced for the bumpers. Low-mileage cars first registered in 1990 probably represent the best value for money available amongst small sportscars.

The tail of the car was finished-off with a spoiler of dubious aerodynamic effect.

A well-trimmed and colourful interior makes the Gran Finale a very attractive package. Note the return to a more sensible gear-lever knob.

Lighting-up time for a 1500 and a Gran Finale.

The signs of a master coachbuilder appear on the bonnet and on the front wings of the X1/9.

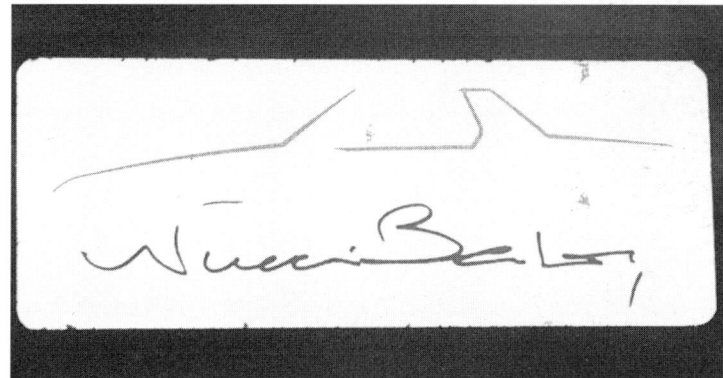

The rear pillars on the Gran Finale are clean and unadorned by the traditional X1/9 logo.

CHAPTER 5

X1/9 on the road

Performance comparisons with rival sportscars

The first X1/9s to appear in Great Britain, apart from some personal imports, were the right-hand-drive cars converted by the Fiat dealers, Radbourne Racing, in 1974. This enterprising company managed to pre-empt the official factory version which would not arrive until 1977, Radbourne taking the initiative to satisfy the public demand for the new sportscar while Fiat were concentrating on the American market.

Although Radbourne were quick to capitalize on Fiat's failure to exploit the British market, the cost of converting the X1/9 meant that the sales price was quite high. Nevertheless, they were able to attract customers to the car because of its exclusivity and curiosity value, and about 30 people were convinced.

The new left-hand-drive X1/9s were imported by Radbourne from the Continent, then, after conversion with the use of 128 components, they were sold as secondhand cars with a delivery mileage. Radbourne would supply either a left-hand-drive car at £2,250 or the converted model for £2,500. They also offered an optional top gear ratio of 1.041:1 to close the gap between third and fourth gears, a situation that was exaggerated by the fitment of the stylish 51/2J x 13 Cromodora alloy wheels and 165HR-13 tyres.

In comparing the converted X1/9 with other sportscars available at the time, cost had to be a key factor, and in the Fiat's price range there were some fairly exclusive cars which, inevitably, were substantially quicker than the small-engined Fiat. For example, there was the Datsun 260Z, which admittedly was considerably more expensive at £2,896, but

the Jensen-Healey was cheaper at £2,420 and the MGB GT V8 cost about the same as the Fiat at £2,508.

Not surprisingly, when *Motor* magazine road-tested Radbourne's demonstrator they criticized the performance-per-pound ratio; but in the exclusivity stakes it was also let down by its poor detail finish. Where it did excel was in the handling department; it was considered to be exceptional in this respect, and the car was praised for its high cornering power. The quality of the gearchange was also appreciated, as were the clever provision of luggage space and the car's fuel economy.

In 1977, when Fiat finally decided to introduce its own right-hand-drive X1/9, the car was priced at £2,998 which, although numerically a higher value than the Radbourne conversion, really meant a price reduction after allowing for inflation. The different price bracket meant that the X1/9 now had some more realistic competitors, several of them being more directly comparable in terms of cost and performance.

Amongst the opposition, the X1/9 stood alone in offering a modern alternative to the ageing selection of available British soft-tops. Its individual design was quite dramatic when compared with the more traditional and conservative vehicles offered for sale in 1977; there was simply nothing else in its class. The X1/9 brought civilization to sportscar motoring without compromising the traditional definition of the concept.

A curious selection of British sportscars were on the market, each one offering certain individual attributes that collectively might have combined to create an ideal car.

From British Leyland, into which the former products of the British Motor Corporation and Standard-Triumph had been integrated following the various takeovers, the cars considered to be the most direct rivals to the Fiat X1/9 were the MG Midget and MGB, and the Triumph Spitfire and TR7. Additionally, there was the independently produced Caterham Super 7, but this was a no-compromise sportscar; effectively it was a racing car made road-legal, and consequently its superb performance was offset by its very limited creature comforts and practicality.

Of the Leyland products, only the Triumph TR7 was a relatively new design which, like the X1/9, had a modern overhead-camshaft engine. The other cars were very long in the tooth, being based on Fifties technology, derived in the main from mainstream saloon models, and suffering from the associated performance characteristics. The TR7 did at least look modern, but it fell short of the fundamental requirement of all 'real' sportscars; it had a fixed roof. The build quality was also the subject of criticism, and it was a noisy car to drive, a situation more acceptable on an open car than a closed coupe. Honour for the TR7 was only restored when Leyland eventually introduced a version that was fully convertible.

The MG and other Triumph models, while technically inferior to the TR7 and X1/9, at least offered the saving grace of full open-air motoring and a very strong fun element. The Spitfire had the additional advantage of amazing under-bonnet access for servicing and repair, the front of the car being a one-piece structure which hinged forward to reveal almost all the engine and suspension components.

The MG Midget was cramped and the MGB was slow, but despite these shortcomings any MG had the benefit of the marque's cult status, and these cars, the MGB in particular, were driven with great flair and enthusiasm by the cloth cap and woolly hat brigade.

Many of the original X1/9 owners were of a very different personality, who bought the car because of its trendy Italian good looks that complemented their own appearance; for them it was to become a fashionable accessory, and as a result in some quarters the X1/9 became branded – not entirely fairly – as the hairdresser's car.

Despite the reluctance of the traditional British sportscar enthusiast to accept change to a more modern concept, the new Fiat had a lot to offer. Most notable were the X1/9's aforementioned road manners, which set new standards, the exceptionally responsive and well-balanced handling, and the car's very high cornering power. The result was very little body roll, and a certain amount of low-speed understeer, which could eventually be converted into high-speed oversteer if the car was pushed sufficiently hard. The steering and braking complemented the handling, the ride was very good and not at all compromised by a suspension system which had been designed specifically for performance purposes. The X1/9 could be driven quickly, safely and well within the limitations of the average driver.

Considering its size, the car is very roomy thanks to the very clever utilization of the available space; the well-equipped cockpit looks more cramped than is actually the case. It was apparent that Bertone had placed a great deal of thought into practicality and driver requirements. The ample luggage space provided in both front and rear compartments, and the novel removable roof section that could be stowed in the front boot, traditionally the home for the spare wheel – which had found its way to a stowage area immediately behind the passenger's seat – were widely appreciated features.

However, despite the attraction of these innovations, the original X1/9s suffered from a lack of general refinement. The general build quality was not particularly inspiring, the doors in particular feeling flimsy and tinny. A minor irritation left over from the implementation of right-hand drive was that the bonnet and boot releases were not moved from the nearside door pillar, which meant that the driver was required to lean across the passenger's seat to operate them.

Wind noise was considered to be excessive and, combined with poor engine noise suppression, this could become tiring over a long journey. The willing 1,290cc engine did not generate the kind of sound that might well be agreeably tolerated in, say, a Lamborghini Miura! It was generally agreed by road-testers that, while the apparently unburstable

Performance comparisons – X1/9 1300					
	Fiat	Midget	MGB	Spitfire	TR7
Cost (£)	2,998	2,085	2,843	2,359	3,335
Capacity (cc)	1,290	1,493	1,798	1,493	1,998
Power (bhp)	73/6,000	65/5,500	84/5,250	71/5,500	105/5,500
Torque (lb.ft)	71.6/3,400	76.5/3,000	102/2,500	82/3,000	118.7/3500
Average mpg	34.4	29	29	35.4	28
Max speed (mph)	97.1	96.5	106.2	98.5	111.2
0–60mph	12.2	11.9	11.5	11.6	9.6

engine was commendably economical and could be stirred up with the excellent gearbox ratios and gearchange, the capacity needed an increase.

The overall conclusions were that although the X1/9 was expensive for a 1300, it offered only moderate performance per pound and it suffered from poor detail finish. However, it was judged to be far more stylish and fun to drive than its rivals. It demanded to be driven fast, with flair and panache, an essential for Italian sportscars. In other words, it had brio.

A new engine was developed to accompany the introduction of the Lancia Delta and Fiat Strada ranges in late 1978. At the same time the X1/9 was updated and fitted with this new 1,498cc unit. When the two-seater was fitted with the larger engine, the motoring press were appreciative of the extra power it provided, reporting that the car had received the performance that it deserved. With the extra 12bhp came greater torque, making the X1/9 easier to drive, and now, with five gears to choose from, there was always some 'go'. The slick new gearbox also assisted in preserving the reputation for economy of the earlier car. The fuel consumption had not been compromised by the capacity increase and the car remained very economical despite the increased performance.

The handling remained superb, being broadly the same as with the 1300 except that the extra overall weight reduced the X1/9's ultimate capability. The brakes remained excellent, so too the ride, which in fact if anything was enhanced due to the improved sprung-to-unsprung ratio. Although the 1500 was heavier, the running gear weighed the same, which had the same effect as reducing the unsprung weight.

Performance comparisons – X1/9 1500					
	Fiat	Midget	MGB	Spitfire	TR7
Cost (£)	4,575	2,971	3,996	3,365	4,764
Capacity (cc)	1,498	1,493	1,798	1,493	1,998
Power (bhp)	85/6,000	65/5,500	97/5,500	71/5,500	105/5,500
Torque (lb.ft)	86.8/3,200	76.5/3,000	104.8/2,500	82/3,000	119/3,500
Average mpg	34	29	29	35.4	31.4
Max speed (mph)	107.1	96.5	106.2	98.5	111.2
0–60mph	9.9	11.9	11.5	11.8	9.6

A pair of X1/9s being evaluated, in this instance a 1984 VS with a silver roof and an all-black 1987-revised VS.

Changes to the interior included better instruments, and there was now a glove locker; altogether, the revised specification added up to an excellent small sportscar, which was more civilized, modern and comfortable than the earlier version. It was great fun and, with its detachable roof, was practical to live with. However, a major criticism of the earlier model remained: it was still a noisy car.

Still rivals

The original competitors of the X1/9 remain rivals in the classic car market. The X1/9 can still offer a considerable degree of exclusivity, providing the car is presented in good condition, of course! The 1300s are pure, original and simple. The interior, though dated, is classic Seventies, with its colourful deckchair-striped seats.

However, a good, original, early X1/9 is now difficult to find, although those that do surface intact will have had a fairly comfortable life and are usually good value for money. Thankfully, the X1/9 had a long production run and many pristine late cars are still available; because of this a

collector's premium is not attached to the price.

The prospective purchaser should buy the best possible car for the money available. Cheap cars must be scrutinized carefully for signs of poor repairs and corroded metal; it is for this reason that the X1/9 as a restoration project loses out to other models. Also, original Fiat body panels tend to be both rare and expensive.

On the other hand, mechanically, the X1/9 is a good prospect, with most components being readily available. Fiat's policy of interchangeability and ease of servicing ensures that new parts are relatively inexpensive and of good quality. Because the major systems components of the X1/9 were of a thoroughly modern and efficient design, the cars are practical to maintain to a satisfactory standard. Maintenance, repair and restoration are covered in greater detail in the next two chapters.

Although originally criticized as a noisy car to drive, the X1/9 today is probably no worse than most of its restored competitors in this respect. There are many convertibles running around these days with poor quality or badly fitted replacement soft-tops that drum and flap. At least the X1/9 owner is saved from this restoration expense, which is unavoidable on conventional open sportscars.

Most British cars have the benefit in the UK of cheaper insurance than the X1/9, an unfortunate situation which is all too familiar when purchasing Italian machinery. If the prospective purchaser is young, but determined to buy an Italian sportscar, the alternative Fiat 128 3P does at least offer a practical compromise until age and experience have been accumulated. Almost certainly the 3P will be cheaper to insure, as well as being faster, more economical and roomier, and having at least some degree of street credibility.

It is always sensible advice to recommend anyone seeking to run an older car to join at least one of the relevant car clubs associated with it. At the time of writing, considerable rivalry seems to exist between the various Fiat clubs in the UK, which is to be regretted because a greater degree of solidarity and co-operation between them would probably attract more support from the manufacturer and better deals from the suppliers of remanufactured panels. A list of useful addresses will be found in the rear of the book.

CHAPTER 6

Practical maintenance and repair – 1

Bodywork and interior

The reputation for corrosion causing the premature demise of many early Seventies' Italian cars is well known. The X1/9 was not immune from this state of affairs and suffered accordingly. Throughout its long production life some of its years of manufacture seem to have provided better quality cars than others, although there is no hard and fast rule about this. In common with all sportscars, when it comes to assessing the car's condition and potential further durability, much depends on the type of use, abuse, storage and the mileage incurred. It may be cold comfort for the X1/9 owner to know that the latest Fiat models are among the finest quality cars in their class currently on the market.

The reason Italian metal deteriorated so quickly has been attributed to a number of factors, including the use of poor-quality materials, inadequate construction procedures and inferior rust-proofing techniques. Yet there was also another reason, of which the unsuspecting prospective new car buyer was probably unaware.

During the Seventies, industrial strife was prevalent throughout the world, many manufacturing companies being crippled by strikes. Italy had its share of these troubles, and the often complicated procedures by which Fiat cars were produced made them particularly vulnerable to this type of disruption.

Traditionally, bodyshells constructed by the coach-builders, like Pininfarina and Bertone, were despatched to the Fiat factories for completion. Any interruption of the assembly lines at either factory often led to unpainted or unprotected bodyshells being left outside to weather the elements. However, the problem cannot be blamed entirely on the Italian manufacturers. Completed cars were often stored for extended periods on salty dockyards and in waterlogged fields, the victims of transportation strikes and inadequate importer facilities.

Bearing these unfavourable circumstances in mind, the prospective X1/9 owner should think very seriously about which model to purchase. Fortunately, X1/9 prices are relatively low compared with those of other comparative sports-cars, but in general 'you get what you pay for'. The search for a good example at a lower price is likely to be much longer and more frustrating than paying a little more for an easier to locate, newer model. The high cost of restoration involving the purchase of scarce, expensive body panels is difficult to justify when very low-mileage, immaculate Gran Finales are still available.

Most pre-1977 X1/9s will have faded away long ago unless they have received substantial restoration. The last Fiat-assembled cars of 1981 and 1982 appear to have survived better than the early 1982 to 1984 Bertone-built models. A comforting fact about the X1/9 is that most of the problem areas are easy to see, so there should be no excuse for anyone being misled into purchasing a bad car. What you see is what you get, but repairing corroded areas, in some cases, is not so straightforward.

Prevalent rust areas in the main are those associated with most cars, namely front and rear wings at the lower corners where they attach to the sills, the outer sills themselves, the rear wheelarch edges, and the front and rear lower valances

This detached front wing may appear to be repairable, but beware the horrors lurking behind, particularly inside the wheelarch.

Rear wheelarch corrosion does not seem to be a major rust area on the X1/9, but in any case can be repaired with a repair section.

Major repair work will be required to rebuild the front suspension pickup points, although access from within the front luggage compartment is very good.

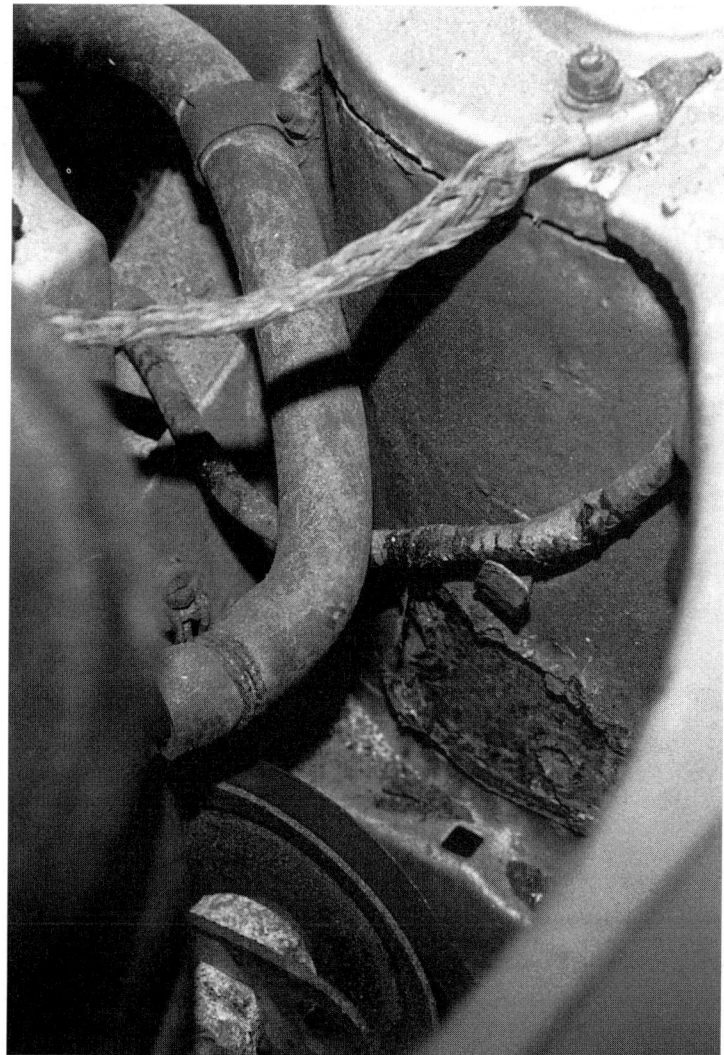

Rear suspension towers are triple-skinned and require high-quality reinforcing. Inevitably, access is severely limited with the engine in place.

A car with substantial corrosion on the windscreen surround should be viewed with suspicion. Permanent repair to this structural area will require the removal of the windscreen.

Deterioration of the front panel may appear spectacular, but it can be replaced with a proprietary replacement panel.

beneath the bumpers. Fortunately, the inner sills and floorpan, except in real basket cases, are not badly affected. Pattern sills are available, and the Fiat sill includes the door surround. Typically, the cost of a sill repair at the time of writing is about £250 per side. It should be noted that occasionally, replacement panels, even genuine factory items, may not be a particularly good fit.

Structural areas requiring more major surgery include the bases of the front and rear shock absorber towers. The corrosion damage can be difficult and expensive to repair because the metalwork in these areas is triple-skinned. Evidence of the corrosion can be seen from within the front luggage and rear engine compartments and, even if the rust appears slight, the true extent of the damage may be considerable. In the same area, the rear suspension pick-up points and the top of chassis legs may require attention. The front wings usually survive quite well, thanks to the protection from stone damage provided by plastic wheelarch liners.

Secondhand engine covers are difficult to locate and are a very complicated fabrication, but glass-fibre replicas offer an alternative solution.

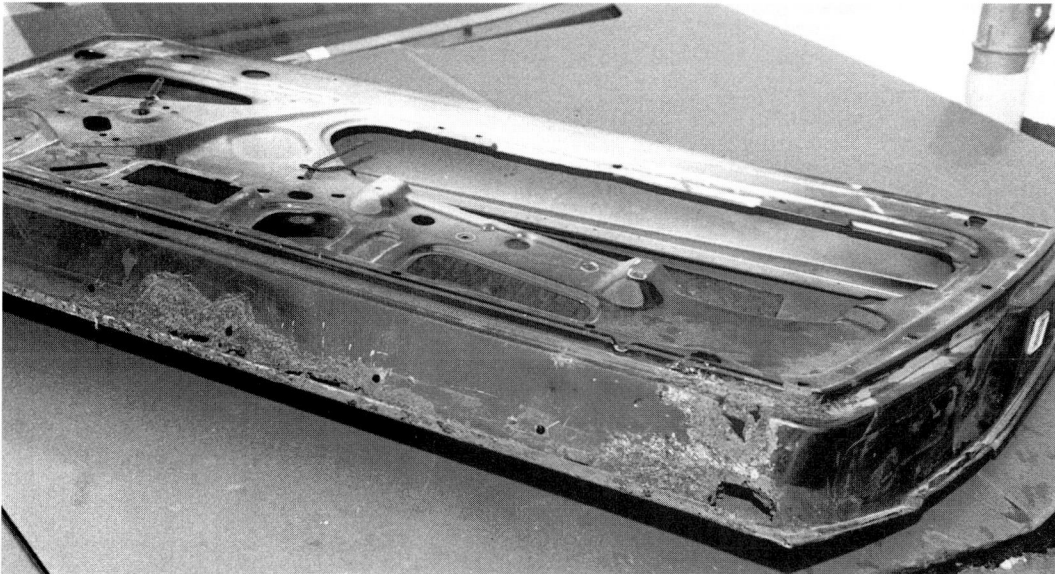

It is possible to repair damaged doors with repair sections. Correct alignment of the new metal is important to provide an accurate run for the window winder mechanism.

Windscreen surrounds can corrode badly, and are notoriously difficult to repair; almost certainly this task will require the removal of the windscreen. Sometimes the rust is generated by the unprofessional screen repairer who slices the rubber seal with a sharp knife and cuts into, and exposes, the metalwork. It goes without saying that an open-top car needs a strong windscreen surround to protect its occupants in the event of an accident.

Front nosecones often rust through in a spectacular fashion, but replacement panels are obtainable. The rear luggage compartment lid and the engine cover both deteriorate, the latter being a complicated fabrication and difficult to source. Occasionally, secondhand panels become available, but these are now in short supply. The inspection panel, hidden behind the carpet in the rear boot, may also require renewal.

New doors are now hard to locate and consequently they tend to be premium-priced.

Removal of the front wing exposes the complicated area that contains the motor to drive the headlight elevating mechanism. Inevitably, electrical problems are likely to occur if damp is allowed access.

The rear boot has an engine access panel that is normally hidden with carpeting.

Doors are the most common difficulty and are consequently highly prized in good condition. They rust from the bottom up, and although pattern and genuine skins are available, the door frame is not. The would-be restorer often discovers that there is nothing to which to attach his door skin. A new door can cost as much as £450. Rusty hinge posts are also a problem when they weaken and allow the door to sag.

The pop-up headlamps have cause to be criticized, and electrical problems are immediately obvious to the observer when the car becomes 'one-eyed'. The headlamp pivots need to be well lubricated to avoid metal stress as overload will cause the expensive elevating motors to fail.

Most doors require repairs along the lower edge and new metal must be let in.

Interior trim

The Bertone VS had the benefit of leather upholstery, which is both hard-wearing and attractive. The other models had fabric material, which wears like any other frequently used soft seating. Light colours were used, which doesn't help to keep the seats clean, especially difficult in this respect being the white Alcantara fitted in the Lido. Of course, it is possible to have the upholstery recovered, and there are plenty of specialist companies able to match materials. However, it is difficult to reproduce the striped 'deck chair' appearance of the early 1300s.

Facias survive well enough and should not be a problem unless the car has been imported from a hot country. Although many cars went to the West Coast of the United States, the relatively low cost of X1/9s in Europe means that there has not been a flood of re-imports from the USA because the price differential does not provide importers with a sufficient profit margin, unlike, for example, the Fiat 124 Spider.

The removable hardtop is normally a good fit, so if there are water leaks into the cabin when driving in rain, it is possible that the car may have suffered some structural damage and undergone repair work.

Arguably, one of the least useful extras fitted to the modern car is a set of electric windows. All vehicles fitted with this device may be fine when new, but when the vehicle ages and the mechanism becomes unreliable, it is both difficult to work on and expensive to replace. The inconvenience suffered can be unbearable if the window fails in the open or partly open position.

The window winding mechanism can cause the owner a

Retrimming of the interior will almost certainly be required on some cars, and there are some high-quality kits on the market. Note the unusual anti-clockwise rev-counter which is standard on the X1/9.

great deal of grief. Anyone who has attempted to replace a cable assembly will be acutely aware of the tangle and mess if the job goes wrong. The secret is to keep the cable tightly wound around the drum until the unit is fully installed. It doesn't help if the door has been 'repaired' at some point and the pulleys are out of alignment. The window has an adjustable rubber stop to limit the upward travel, and if this is not adjusted properly or it deteriorates, the window will catch on the roof. Access to the stop is obtained by removing the interior courtesy light mounted in the door panel.

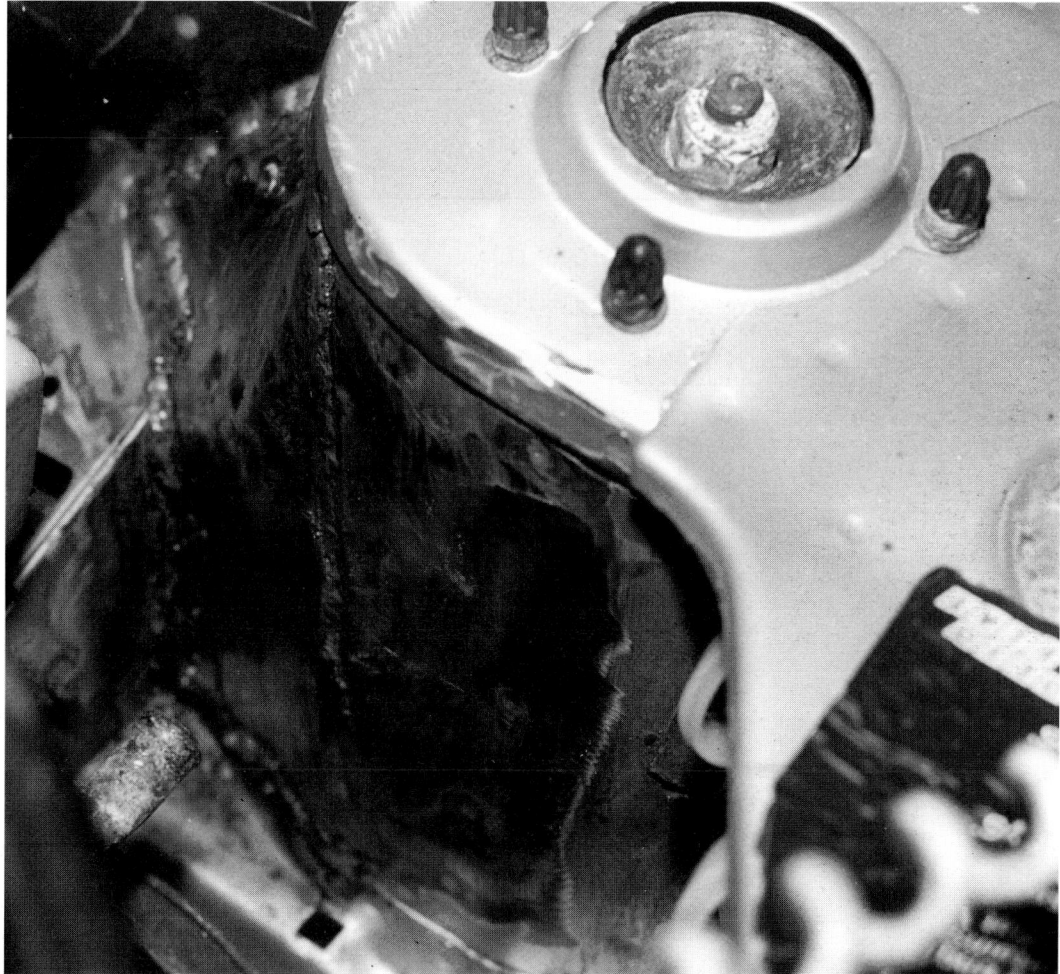

The rear suspension turrets are a load-bearing structure and need substantial reinforcement.

Rear wings can normally be refurbished provided the rust is not too extensive.

The lower trailing edge of the rear wing is an area that frequently requires attention.

CHAPTER 7

Practical maintenance and repair – 2

Engine, transmission and chassis components

Although cars with a mid-engine configuration have a reputation for inaccessibility when servicing and repair work becomes necessary, the X1/9 has been thoughtfully designed with the convenience of the mechanic in mind. Routine tasks are not as difficult as they may first appear, thanks to the provision of access panels, which can be removed to reach such components as, for example, the distributor and the crankshaft pulley.

Properly maintained, the X1/9 engine will have a life well in excess of 100,000 miles. However, oil changes must never be overlooked, otherwise there is a risk of the oilways in the camshaft becoming gummed up; this inevitably will accelerate wear and in extreme cases can cause the camshaft to tighten, strip the cam belt and cause the valves to hit the pistons. Care should be taken when draining the oil because the sump on the X1/9 is made from alloy and it is possible to damage the threads on the drain plug hole.

Cam belt replacement
Apart from changing the oil, replacing the cam belt is probably the most important servicing task. The X1/9 engine is not 'failsafe' in the sense that if the relationship between the camshaft and crankshaft is disturbed, the valves will touch the pistons. This unhappy situation can result if a worn cam belt slips or breaks, the consequences then being potentially disastrous. The mechanic needs to be aware that the valves can also touch the pistons while the pulleys are being aligned during the manual valve timing operation; over-enthusiastic rotation of the pulleys will create the undesired contact.

Fiat recommend that the belt be changed every 36,000 miles, but in my opinion, to be on the safe side it is advisable to replace it earlier, especially if the car is used mainly in town. City driving should be assessed in hours rather than recorded miles! In any event, it is sensible to change the belt as soon as possible after buying the car; do not rely on doubtful servicing records.

To replace the belt the engine should be rotated to the point where all the timing marks coincide – this is on the assumption that the timing is correct in the first place. Before removing the belt cover, highlight the timing marks with paint. The 1300 has reference marks on the plastic cam belt cover; the 1500 has a pointer attached to the block. If possible, mark the relationship of the pulley against some static structure like the chassis: this is useful because the crankshaft has little mechanical resistance and will move freely about the top dead centre point. This procedure will avoid having to temporarily refit the cover to check the marks. On both engine types there are additional reference marks on the flywheel, access to which is via an inspection hole in the gearbox bellhousing.

There are also reference marks available to set the camshaft pulley; one is a pointer fixed on top of the rear cam belt shield, the other forms part of the water pump casting in the '7 o'clock' position of the cam wheel. Some 1500 engines do not have the cam wheel inscribed with a mark to coincide with this marker. It is advisable for the mechanic to mark this himself because it is very easy to set the cam pulley 180deg

Perhaps not very glamorous, but nevertheless significant, the Bertone 'Shake' was the factory development vehicle for the X1/9 project.

The Runabout, although presented at the Turin Show in 1969 as an Autobianchi 'dream car', was in fact a study prototype for the X1/9.

A 1972 car. One of the very first production X1/9s. The appearance is pure but the 4½J steel wheels do little to enhance its looks.

The first all-Bertone X1/9 was the 1982 'IN'. This very attractive colour scheme included a silver roof.

out of synchronization. Fortunately, the valves will not touch if this error occurs and the engine will not start.

Ignition system

Observe the relative positions between the rotor arm and the distributor cap. With the engine set in the valve timing position, it is important to note that the ignition is timed to fire on number 4 piston, not number 1. It is worth noting the rotor arm position because it is inevitable that the auxiliary drive pulley, which drives the distributor, will be disturbed during the cam belt change.

When the mechanic is satisfied that the timing is perfect, the cam belt tensioner should be released and then locked off in the fully slack position. Cut through the old belt to avoid it being re-used accidentally. Fit the new belt, being careful not to trap or crease it. It will be observed that one part of the belt will be more slack than the other, so the tensioner will now need to be set. With the HT leads disconnected, turn the engine over at least three times and release and reset the tensioner on each occasion. There will always be some inequality where the belt tension is tighter in one stage of engine rotation than another. Lock off the tensioner when a compromise has been achieved. Never over-tighten the belt to the point where there is no slack at all.

Before an attempt is made to start the engine, recheck the timing marks. Set the distributor to the point where the rotor arm is almost in line with number 4 contact on the cap. It is possible that the rotation of the auxiliary shaft has moved the distributor into a position where it has become difficult to access the screws securing the cap, or access the points for adjustment. If this is the case the whole distributor will need to be lifted out of its mount, rotated and refitted to a position where access is improved.

With the rotor arm and cap aligned as described, remove number 4 spark plug. Turn the ignition on and move the distributor until the plug sparks. Refit the spark plug and retighten the clamp securing the distributor. The engine should now start. If it doesn't, either the ignition or the valve timing is out, or perhaps both! As a handy hint to assist a confused mechanic, the position of the valves can easily be observed by blowing down the appropriate plug hole with a suitable piece of pipe. When number 4 piston is on its firing stroke, infinite resistance will be encountered, whereas in any other position the air blown down the pipe will flow through the valves. Provided the cylinder is confirmed to be on its firing stroke and there is an accompanying spark, the engine should fire.

Distributors require frequent attention and the points adjustment should be monitored regularly. Deposits on the points face will close up the gap and cause poor starting and loss of power. The gap will also close up as the fibre heel wears down, usually accelerated by the distributor cam not being adequately greased. The contacts in the distributor cap and rotor arm deteriorate or crack, then the condenser breaks down and burns the contact face of the points. Eventually the insulation of the HT leads will also break down, causing arcing between the cables, shorting-out on metalwork and generally diminishing the spark to the plugs. A failed oil seal on the distributor spindle may also allow oil to contaminate the points. A veritable minefield of potential faults! It is obvious, therefore, that replacing all these easily obtainable, regular service parts before proceeding any further will form a sound basis from which to progress.

Distributors on the very early X1/9s were fitted to the end of the camshaft, but most owners are likely to have their cars fitted with the crankcase-mounted version, access to which is through a panel behind the spare wheel.

Cooling system

Cooling faults are exaggerated by the X1/9's rear-engined design, and any defects in the system will inevitably lead to overheating and subsequent engine damage. Ensure that all hoses and unions are in good condition; if any hoses become soft or swell they must be changed.

The steel transfer pipes which carry water from the front-mounted radiator to the engine run under the floor in a tunnel. If they corrode and split due to lack of anti-freeze, their repair is extremely difficult and expensive. The pipes are completely inaccessible inside a box section that forms part of the floorpan structure, so any surgery in this area is major. An all-year-round anti-freeze solution of a 50 per cent mixture is advised to avoid this problem; it also reduces corrosion and the build-up of sludge throughout the cooling system.

The plastic expansion tank may become brittle and split, no doubt due to its proximity to the exhaust system. The original 1300 had the benefit of a steel tank and would be a suitable prize if sourced from a scrapped car.

Air locks in the cooling system's extended pipework should be attended to; the radiator has a bleed screw on its top left corner, access to which is found under the bonnet and requires an 8mm Allen key. When refilling the system, ensure that the heating controls are set to allow water to flow through the heater radiator.

There are some simple clues to observe that forewarn the owner of impending doom. The sudden loss of temperature from the cabin heater, caused by lack of water, pre-empts an overheat situation. Also, if the expansion tank is suddenly observed to be full of water after a run, and then subsides after the car has cooled down, this is another warning sign. Inevitably, untreated symptoms will lead to a blown head gasket. This may not happen immediately, but the following telltale signs will provide an indication of what will occur:

1) Regular topping-up of the expansion tank without visual water leaks.
2) Gurgling noises within the cooling system.
3) Water vapour appearing from the exhaust system that continues after the engine reaches full running temperature.
4) Radiator cooling fan does not cut in.
5) Emulsified oil slime on the underside of the oil filler cap.
6) The car starts on three or less cylinders then clears to run normally.

If all this is happening, the cylinder head needs to be removed without delay before any terminal damage occurs.

Cylinder head

In the event of head gasket failure, always machine the cylinder head surface because the overheating will almost certainly have warped the aluminium casting. It requires discipline by the mechanic in not being tempted to cut corners here, for simply replacing the gasket without skimming the head is a very short-term and unprofessional solution.

Refitting the cylinder head should be carried out with extreme care. The gasket must sit evenly on the block surface and the head gently lowered onto the locating dowels. The head bolts must be tightened exactly to the manufacturer's prescribed method and torque settings.

Cylinder head removal may prove to be difficult on early engines which were fitted with nuts securing the cylinder head onto steel studs. The studs often seize in the aluminium head. Later engines had an improved design where the studs were replaced by bolts.

Valve clearances should be checked at the prescribed intervals. On overhead-camshaft engines the clearances reduce with wear, unlike with pushrod engines, where they increase and result in noisy tappets. If uncorrected, reduced clearances will eventually lead to the valves not seating properly and ultimately becoming burnt.

Electrics

Alternators are often criticized for being the cause of electrical malaise, but if treated with respect they should survive a very high mileage. An alternator is far more reliable than the old-style dynamo and has fewer working parts, and therefore requires little maintenance.

Faults are more likely to occur because of indifferent servicing. Basic procedures, like correct drive belt tension, are extremely important. If the belt is too tight, the alternator bearings will become stressed, causing eventual failure, a problem which will also affect the water pump, which shares the same belt. Under-tension will cause the belt to slip and shriek, the alternator will then not run at the correct speed and the battery will not receive adequate charging and so eventually will become flat.

Unlike the brushes of a dynamo, those of an alternator can be replaced without major dismantling. The brush pack is conveniently mounted on the end of the alternator and is retained by two screws. The need to change the brushes will normally be accompanied by a lack of charging or the ignition warning light on the dash will illuminate. If the warning light remains on after the brush pack has been changed, it is possible that a diode will have failed, a fault

One of the early Bertone-badged cars. This one is duo-tone metallic blue; others were silver over black, champagne over brown, red over black and all black.

Customized X1/9s at an international X1/9 meeting at the Nurburgring.

The Dallara X1/9 was prepared for competition under 'silhouette' regulations that permitted the use of front and rear spaceframes. The dramatic weight reduction and powerful engine produced a very competitive car.

which may be accompanied by headlights that vary in brightness according to engine speed. It is impractical for the mechanic to replace a faulty diode, and in this event a replacement alternator should be sought. The alternator on the X1/9 should be covered by a shield to protect the unit from road wash.

Starting problems are often blamed on carburation faults, but it is easy to overlook simple defects like a detached or corroded earthing strap. Often its replacement is forgotten if the transmission has been removed. Because the power unit is mounted in the body by rubber bushing, the earthing strap is necessary for the electrics to be effective. The symptoms are rapid battery discharge, even with a new battery, and irregular failure of the starter motor to turn over the engine.

Fuel system

Starting difficulties and running problems such as misfires and a lack of power are very often ignition-related. Any faults that occur should be addressed by a thorough check of the ignition system before any attempt is made to alter the carburation; ignition maintenance should always be considered the first stage of fault-finding as it can save a lot of wasted time. If the fuel system is adjusted first and then the fault is eventually traced to the ignition, the fuel system will need to be attended to all over again.

The X1/9 has an inherent fuel vaporization problem that is exaggerated by lack of maintenance of the fuel system. Restricted ventilation in the engine bay and the fact that the carburettor sits immediately above the exhaust manifold are the root causes of the problem. To address it, Fiat installed a fan to cool the carburettor. However, often this fails to operate, either because it seizes up, or the temperature switch becomes defective. The feeble tubular trunking is easily damaged or dislodged, so even if the fan is operating the air may be misdirected.

To minimize the effects of fuel vaporization efficient carburettor maintenance is essential. An in-line transparent fuel filter should be installed to monitor the quality of the petrol; any sediment or water from the tank will become apparent. There is also a filter in the carburettor cover, which can be accessed without difficulty. The mechanical fuel pump itself is normally reliable, but it is worth remembering that it is cheap and easily replaced; changing it removes another area of doubt!

The type of carburettor fitted to the X1/9 is vulnerable to variations in the float level. The needle valve tends to wear, so a small investment here could be rewarding. The effect of a worn valve will be fuel flooding. If the floats are out of adjustment, a low fuel level will exaggerate the fuel starvation situation and lead to erratic running or stalling.

To check the adjustment, remove the top of the carburettor, but do so carefully so to avoid damaging the gasket, which can be re-used. It is advisable to disconnect the fuel pipes, any choke linkages and the jets to allow the cover to be raised gently and vertically off the carb.

Measurements are taken with the gasket fitted and with the tongue on the float arm just touching, but not depressing, the ball on the needle valve. Make sure that both floats are equally adjusted. Most instruments require the upper level to be from 6.75mm to 7mm and the lower measurement in all cases is 15mm.

Before replacing the cover carrying the floats, check the surface for flatness. The cover is easily distorted and dangerous fuel leaks may occur. Tighten the screws down diametrically. Damaged gaskets on the carb base or on the cylinder head will allow air or water leaks and affect the smooth running at tickover.

Only after all ignition and fuel system checks have been carried out should the fuel/air mixture be adjusted. If all the adjustments mentioned have been performed efficiently, the mixture and tickover will be easy to set. In an ideal world this is how it should happen:

1) Bring the engine up to normal operating temperature.
2) Set an idle speed of about 1,000rpm.
3) Adjust the mixture screw inwards until the engine speed just begins to falter.
4) Adjust outwards until the engine speed rises, and then stabilizes.
5) Reset the tickover to about 950rpm.

If the tickover note rises on its own, becomes lumpy,

erratic or stalls the engine, the mechanic should recheck all of the above.

Carburettor types vary, but most will have the water temperature-operated automatic choke. Some owners regard this system with suspicion, and it does require some adjustment. Setting it up is a nuisance because it relies on a cold engine to do so. It is very tedious to adjust each cold morning, for a week, before setting off for work … on the assumption that the car starts.

Early 1300s had a manual choke, the cable of which could break somewhere in the depths of the transmission tunnel. Manual carbs can be sourced from other cars, Fiat or Lancia, which have the same manifold mounting studs.

A very useful installation was the fitment, from 1980, of Bosch Jetronic fuel injection on cars for the American market. This system solved the fuel vaporization problems associated with the carburettor and provided a useful power increase as well. Unfortunately, this desirable installation is not easily sourced in Britain.

Emissions

Now that statutory vehicle emissions checks are with us, it is more important than ever to maintain a clean engine. Also, an engine that runs cleanly will be both more efficient and more economical. However, if the CO content of the exhaust is excessive, the matter cannot be rectified by simply weakening-off the carburettor fuel/air mixture. Dirty engines can be attributed to the lack of a relatively simple, but all too often overlooked, servicing operation: cleaning the crankcase breather.

The breather is designed to relieve the pressure in the crankcase created by the pumping action of the pistons. The pressure is vented through the breather pipe to the carburettor and back into the engine. A fine oil mist is trapped within the breather swirl pot and builds up with mileage to form sludge. The sludge eventually restricts the airflow and clogs the wire flame trap in the breather pipe. The effect is to restrict the airflow to the carburettor, which will alter the fuel/air mixture. Failure to service the breather, or to replace a collapsed pipe, will allow the crankcase pressure to build up and force itself out elsewhere, usually through various seals. The result will almost certainly be a choked, dirty, oily engine.

There is a more sinister problem connected with the crankcase breather. If the oil leaks persist, often through the dipstick or oil filler cap seals, and the carburettor air filter becomes clogged, allowing the engine to burn oil, the crankcase may be over-pressurized. This symptom is often the result of a broken piston ring, which is allowing combustion pressure to reach the crankcase. To confirm this unhappy circumstance a compression test should be carried out; any inequality in the readings will indicate the problem cylinder. This test will also reveal defects in valve sealing.

Gearbox

Four-speed gearboxes appear to be more reliable than the later five-speed variety. Poor synchromesh between second and third is a common weakness and the ratios can be noisy and sometimes jump out of mesh. Early five-speed gearboxes had the same selector spring as fitted to the original four-speed 'box, which was not man enough for the extra load imposed on it with the additional gear. Accordingly, later five-speeds were modified.

Another annoying fault is a tendency for some cars to jump out of reverse gear. Some people suggest adjusting the linkage, but this is unlikely to cure the problem, which is thought to be brought about by lack of mechanical sympathy on the part of the driver. When the car is started from cold and on choke, the revs are too high for the non-synchro reverse gear to cope with the forced selection. To concentrate the mind, the cost of an exchange box can be about £400, while a new one can be as much as £1,400.

Removing and refitting the gearbox should not present any major difficulties for the average mechanic. As a precaution to avoid damage, the vulnerable reversing light switch should be removed during work on the gearbox. If possible, identify the age of the five-speed gearbox before ordering spare parts as there are two designs with component variations, in particular differing sizes of ring gears.

If a replacement gearbox is sourced from a Fiat 128 or Strada, the bellhousing will have to be changed over because the clutch operating arm location is reversed.

Speed with style; on test with a Gran Finale and a 1500.

This innocent looking 1988 car is fitted with a powerful turbocharged engine.

A very rare X1/9 Lido in original condition, the only model to carry chromium-plated bumpers.

Driveshafts

The driveshafts and CV joints are very reliable and capable of surviving very high mileages provided that the rubber gaiters are in good condition. Damaged gaiters allow road wash to enter the joint and cause premature wear at an alarming rate.

A regular check on the condition of the gaiters is therefore essential, not only for the life of the CV joints, but also for that of the gearbox. Splits in the inner gaiters will allow the gearbox oil to escape, with very expensive consequences.

The shafts will only need changing when the inner gaiter oil seal wears a groove on its circumference, which can cause a leak. When a new inner seal is being fitted, care should be taken to ensure that the lip has been correctly located on the gearbox housing, otherwise oil will escape. The studs and nuts securing the seal to the gearbox are easily damaged or cross-threaded.

Later 1500 shafts have a more substantial arrangement which does not incorporate an inner gaiter. Instead, an additional CV joint is installed, this being attached to a flange mounted on the gearbox output shaft. If the driveshaft needs to be removed, the mechanic will require a good quality Allen key attachment to fit on the end of a ½in drive ratchet. The Allen bolts that secure the CV joint to the flange must be cleaned of road dirt to allow the key to make adequate contact. Failure to do this will damage both the tool and the bolt, thus making the task more tedious than necessary.

Brakes, suspension and steering

It is essential that extra attention be paid to the condition of the brakes, suspension and steering on the Fiat X1/9. This sportscar demands to be driven hard, and the owner may be lulled into a false sense of security because of the excellent handling quality inherent in its design. The X1/9 driver is likely to operate the car beyond the limits normally experienced with lesser vehicles, sometimes without being aware of it. For this reason, high regard should be paid to the efficient servicing of these three safety-related areas.

All braking system components are readily available. Early 1300s had a 127-style front caliper unit which can be interchanged with the superseding design. The later front calipers are common across a wide range of Fiat models, notably the 124, 125, 128, 131 and 132. The units are relatively inexpensive and may be even cheaper if sourced from FSO and Lada cars, which share the same design. Some Fiat 850 models also have similar calipers, but they should be avoided because the jaws are narrower, preventing the use of the correct thickness of brake pad.

Rear calipers are a different proposition because they are exclusive to the X1/9 and costly. Although the general design is similar to 124 and FSO units, which are cheaper, the pistons are of a reduced diameter. It is possible to install 124, 132 and FSO units with the larger pistons, and some owners claim an increase in braking performance by doing so, but if this modification is chosen, the owner should consider that the manufacturer must have had a very good reason to adopt a different design in the first place. In any event, to avoid an imbalance, calipers with different-sized pistons must not be mixed.

Providing the car is used regularly, high mileages are possible without encountering problems with the braking system. However, if the car has been standing for a long period, the pistons in the calipers may tighten up, or seize altogether. This will become evident when the car pulls to one side under braking. The offending front caliper is always the one on the opposite side to the direction towards which the steering pulls, a situation being caused by one caliper doing more work than the other. Rear caliper problems usually become evident when the handbrake begins to lose overall efficiency or fails to hold one of the road wheels.

Calipers are long-life items providing some care is taken with them. Dust covers should be inspected and replaced if any deterioration or damage is evident. Damp and road wash will quickly corrode the portion of the piston that is exposed by split or perished rubber. Rubber caps should also be fitted to the brake nipples; these are easily lost during the brake bleeding operation.

A sticking piston may be freed temporarily by using the following method:

Front caliper: Dismount the caliper from its carrier, without disturbing the brake hose. Remove the piston dust cover. Place a G-clamp inside the piston recess and over the rear of the caliper housing. Arrange the clamp so that when the brake pedal is depressed the piston will move about an inch out of the housing and bear up against the clamp. Clean the exposed piston surface and smear with petroleum jelly (not grease, which will affect the rubber). Operate the G-clamp to re-insert the piston. Repeat the procedure until the piston moves freely. Re-assemble the brakes and test. If the problem persists, the caliper will require a full strip-down, clean and the fitting of new seals.

Rear caliper: Fully release the handbrake cable adjustment and mount the G-clamp as per the front caliper. Press the piston out via the brake pedal as before, but do not re-insert the piston by operating the G-clamp. A large screwdriver blade should be inserted into the slot across the piston, and the piston screwed back in. Failure to do this will damage the self-adjuster mechanism. The pistons are properly inserted when the machined witness mark is above the slot and horizontal.

Resetting the rear caliper adjusters is also necessary when renewing the brake pads. When changing the pads it is important to release the handbrake cable tension before the adjusters are reset, otherwise handbrake efficiency will be affected. For the same reason the correct procedure for adjusting the handbrake cable must also be followed.

Handbrake adjustment
With the cable fully slackened-off, several firm applications of the brake pedal will reset the self-adjusting mechanism inside the rear calipers. Starting from the fully off position, raise the lever three clicks on the ratchet. Adjust the cable until the road wheels are locked. Release the handbrake lever and check the number of clicks and re-adjust as necessary.

If the handbrake runs out of adjustment after the self-adjusting mechanism has been reset and the brake pads have been changed, a new cable may be required. Cables can seize if they remain unlubricated; the extra effort necessary to apply the handbrake will eventually stretch the cable.

Left and right cables are separate, but should be changed as a pair for balance. The cables are tricky to fit round the pulleys that route them through the tunnel, and it may be found easier to remove the pulley wheels, attach the cable, then replace as an assembly. Afterwards, be sure to grease all the exposed cable.

Brake discs
Resurfacing scored or generally worn brake discs is impractical because new discs are both inexpensive and plentiful. Always fit new pads to new discs. Front and rear brake pads are not interchangeable; the rear pads have a raised metal ridge on the back plate, which is essential for operating the automatic wear adjusting mechanism.

Brake hoses
Often overlooked, and obscured during inspection from underneath the car, are the rubber hoses which supply hydraulic fluid to the brake calipers. The rear hoses are especially prone to splitting caused by the tight routing of the pipework. The split outer braiding leaves the inner tubing vulnerable to damage, but also causes the hose to expand under pressure, the effect of which will be felt through a spongy feeling to the brake pedal and loss of pressure.

If the front hoses are not provided with an unrestricted run or are too short, they will restrict the steering movement or rub on the road wheel; obviously this is dangerous. It is possible that an over-stretched hose will damage the soft inner pipe. The damage may not be evident until an apparently incurable problem manifests itself. The symptoms of the problem are a one-way effect when the brakes are applied and do not release. This occurs because the fluid under pressure is forced through the collapsed pipe, but does not return when the pedal is released, causing the brakes to lock on or bind. It is recommended that, even though the hoses appear to be intact, they should be replaced when the calipers are reconditioned or changed.

When installing new hoses it should be noted that a 14mm spanner will be required, an unusual size and not always in everyone's toolkit. When reassembling the hoses, in order to provide more room for the spanner to be used effectively, the

Accessibility is demonstrated with all panels open. The car is a 1984 X1/9 VS.

1977 Serie Speciale, 1990 Gran Finale and two Eurosport-styled cars at Brooklands.

bleed nipple should be removed to avoid possible damage.

It is much easier to assemble the hoses on a dry caliper before connecting up the hydraulics, rather than correct messy leaks later. Attempting to retighten a brake hose during brake bleeding will wind up the rubber and affect its flexibility. Excess fluid will contaminate the brake pad lining material, rendering the pad useless.

Brake bleeding

It is important to use good quality tools for work on the brakes. Preferably these spanners should be kept to one side and used exclusively when working on the brakes. Bleed nipples ideally require a multi-flat 8mm ring spanner. Worn tools will quickly wear out the flats on the nipple, thus preventing its release or, more probably, will shear it off.

Most calipers are rendered scrap by snapping off the bleed nipples. If the nipples have remained undisturbed for some time they will seize in the caliper, this being caused by dissimilar metal corrosion between the steel nipple and aluminium caliper. Another problem can occur when nipples are over-tightened during the brake bleeding operation; they should only be tightened with just enough effort to prevent leaking fluid.

Whenever a brake caliper is stripped down, the nipples should be wire-brushed, or preferably replaced, if any restriction is evident. They cannot be lubricated effectively because the caustic hydraulic fluid will remove any traces of grease. Anyone who has accidentally spilt fluid on car bodywork will know how caustic it is, and seen its effectiveness as a paint-stripper!

The fluid should be completely changed periodically. It is hydroscopic by nature, which means that it absorbs moisture. A soft pedal will occur if the brakes are used heavily during fast driving, at a club track test day for example. This happens when the water in the brake fluid boils and becomes uncompressible, resulting in the brake pedal going to the floor with a simultaneous loss of brakes. Leaving the car to cool down will restore the pedal pressure, after which bleeding through the fluid will be necessary at the earliest opportunity.

Fluid loss should be viewed with suspicion. If all the unions and seals are intact, a drop in reservoir level may be caused by 'space' in the system through worn brake pads. When the pads are renewed the pistons will need to be pressed back into the calipers; the owner should remember that if the reservoir had been topped up previously, an overflow of fluid is possible.

The bleeding operation is common with most hydraulic systems. It is worth noting that when topping-up the reservoir during bleeding the cap must be replaced each time. It is possible for spillage to occur if anyone stamps on the pedal while checking for pressure.

Brake master cylinder

This unit is positioned above the pedal box in the driver's compartment and is most inconvenient to work on. The brake master cylinder and the clutch master and slave cylinders are exclusive to the X1/9 and can be expensive if obtained from official Fiat spares outlets.

Loss of pedal pressure without any visual evidence of leaks may be due to worn seals in the master cylinder. The rubber seals become damaged because of dirty hydraulic fluid that has remained unchanged for a long period of time. Resealing the cylinder may be effective only in the short term because the bore may have become scored. When reassembling the components, ensure that the pistons are fitted the right way up; this can be checked by assessing the amount of travel by pushing the piston against the spring; the travel should be several inches, otherwise there will be a mechanical restriction, an infinitely hard pedal pressure, and no brakes. To avoid this unpleasant dismantling task recurring, a completely new cylinder and clean brake fluid is the best guarantee of lasting efficiency.

Clutch cylinders

While on the subject of hydraulic cylinders, the clutch on the X1/9 is also hydraulically operated, the rear-engined configuration being unsuitable for the more conventional cable system. Both master and slave cylinders are exclusive to the X1/9.

Complications can arise when the cylinders have been replaced or overhauled and require bleeding. The clutch pedal design allows the linkage to go over-centre if the pedal is pushed to the floor during the bleeding operation. Unfortunately, dismantling is necessary in order to raise the pedal again, which is a great inconvenience and a major irritation. To avoid this it is recommended that a pressure bleeding kit be used, which removes the need to pump the clutch pedal.

Suspension struts

The MacPherson strut system is both reliable and effective. Wear is progressive, and the owner is unlikely to detect any sudden effects requiring urgent replacement of the shock absorbers. Changes in the car's handling balance or excessive body roll are the likely signs that renewal is necessary.

Oil appearing on the shock absorber pistons indicates the need to replace the units. To maintain balance in the handling they should be changed in pairs, ideally all four together.

Wear in the suspension bottom balljoints of the lower wishbone assemblies has an adverse and potentially dangerous effect on the roadholding of the X1/9. The play upsets the rear wheel alignment, allowing it to steer the car. The driver may notice that this undesirable situation is often accompanied by play in the steering wheel and 'clonks' from the rear of the car. The condition of the assembly is difficult to assess without the weight of the car being supported by a hydraulic lift. The balljoint is incorporated in the wishbone assembly and cannot normally be renewed without replacing the entire unit. At the time of writing a new wishbone assembly can cost around £200.

Steering rack

A final point to remember when seeking to maintain the durability and reliability of your X1/9, the steering rack gaiters must be replaced immediately any splits appear, otherwise oil will be lost and the rack-and-pinion gears will wear. If the gaiters are changed with the rack remaining on the car, an oil can with a long spout will be required to force in the oil past the outer seal.

A restorer's nightmare! Accurate reproduction of this unique logo must be very difficult, in fact it is rarely replaced after cars have been repainted.

Improving the breed

Performance and styling conversions

It is very tempting to fall into the trap of categorizing the X1/9 owner. A large cross-section of club members seem to be young and in the early-twenties age group, and apparently of some means to be able to afford the fairly high insurance premiums. On the other hand, a different group of owners are professional women, married couples who use the car for holidays, and retired gentlemen in their seventies.

It would appear that most X1/9 owners are content to just enjoy driving their cars, keeping them in original condition. The average owner is careful to keep their car tidy, treating it with respect; X1/9s are not often seen in poor condition, or being badly driven.

Some use the car as a suitable basis for free expression and carry out customizing and styling changes. While a number of these modifications have been carried out quite tastefully, others are extreme and of dubious success. However, beauty is in the eye of the beholder ... There is another group of owners who prefer to exploit the excellent sporting characteristics of the X1/9 by uprating its specification and injecting varying degrees of increased power into the car. There are, of course, some who combine revised appearance with tuning.

Before any attempt is made to increase the power output of the X1/9 it is essential that all other aspects of the car are carefully considered. Tuning any car requires the uprating of all the mechanical systems to cope with the extra demands imposed on them, not only to improve their performance, but also for the driver's personal safety. It is both useless and dangerous to increase engine power output without paying attention to the brakes, wheels and tyres, suspension and the cooling system. Any alteration to these systems must be proportionate to the level of increased power being sought.

A number of effective conversions can be carried out, the best known being the installation of the Fiat/Lancia twin-cam engine. Turbocharging is another popular course, utilizing Fiat Uno Turbo components. These transplants require considerable engineering expertise, time and resources. However, it is possible for the owner with limited facilities and experience to improve the original engine, either by fitting an uprated exhaust system and air filter and rejetting the carburettor, or by fitting twin carburettors and an improved camshaft.

Twin-cam transplant
The twin-cam engine is usually sourced from the Lancia Beta. Increases of up to 250bhp are entirely possible, but to do so would have a dramatic effect on the appearance of the car, not to mention the amount of finance required in the owner's pocket. Huge power outputs can have a significant effect on the balance of mid-engined cars, while the necessarily wide tyres and stiffer suspension will also have an adverse effect on the car if it is primarily intended for road use.

A good example of the effect on the handling characteristics of a powerful mid-engined car is the behaviour exhibited by the Lancia Stratos. Because of its large power output and short wheelbase (exaggerated by oversize wheels and tyres), the car will spin in its own length without much provocation, especially on wet tarmac. The Stratos is also notoriously difficult to drive in a straight line, which may not be a problem on a twisting forest rally stage, but is a definite nuisance on the North Circular Road.

If the owner wishes to retain the original appearance of the standard X1/9 instead of driving something that looks like the Group 4 Abarth Rallye, a more sensible choice of power level would be up to about 140bhp.

Twin-cam conversions demand professional installation because some chassis surgery is required, and indifferent craftsmanship can severely compromise the structural integrity of the vehicle. A professional engineering approach is required before removing huge chunks from a perfectly serviceable chassis and potentially rendering it unsafe.

The enthusiast who desires a twin-cam X1/9, but lacks the necessary technical experience, might be better off purchasing a car that has already been converted. But it is essential to qualify the effectiveness of the conversion by having the car professionally inspected; a road test should reveal how well the car actually drives.

For the determined engineer, careful sourcing of a twin-cam engine and gearbox is necessary. The angle of inclination of the engine when fitted to the X1/9 is important for ease of installation and carburettor clearance. The early, pre-injection Lancia Beta seems to be the best option.

A standard Beta unit in good condition will produce a rewarding 120bhp. There are several tuning options, varying from twin carburettors and modified camshafts, through to big-valve heads and full race preparation. Mild tuning of the twin-cam is possible for the competent enthusiast because

The search for additional power has led to alternative engines being installed in the X1/9 chassis, the Fiat and Lancia twin-cam being regarded as one of the most suitable. Installation problems influence the inclination of the engine, and this one has been tilted forward, resulting in the sidedraught carburettors being 'buried' in the bulkhead.

Another forward-inclined 2-litre installation; note the distributor driven by the inlet camshaft.

the engine parts are readily available and servicing is user-friendly. For owners choosing to obtain a professionally uprated engine there are several organizations that are capable, most prominent being Guy Croft Tuning.

Turbocharging
An alternative to the twin-cam conversion is the transplanting of a Fiat Uno Turbo engine. Arguably this is the most beneficial option. If an intended power increase between 120 and 140bhp is sought, the Uno Turbo unit offers some advantages: it is lighter than the twin-cam and is therefore less likely to have any detrimental effect on the handling balance, while another benefit is the ease with which the X1/9 mountings accept the power unit without the need for structural surgery.

Either a Mk1 1,301cc or a Mk2 1,367cc Uno Turbo engine is a practical proposition; although superior, the Mk2 unit requires some mix and match of X1/9 and Mk1 Uno components.

Assuming the choice of the Mk2 1,367cc unit, a number of components will require changing. The flywheel must be from the Mk1 and mated to an X1/9 clutch; the Mk2 has a different spline arrangement and the X1/9 flywheel has too many teeth. The X1/9 gearbox casing should be used, preferably with Uno Mk1 internals. The bellhousing will require modification to mount the rpm sensor that acts on the ring gear. The X1/9 engine mountings can be retained along with the standard X1/9 clutch slave cylinder.

An X1/9 cam housing is required with a Uno Mk1 cam cover and throttle linkage. The X1/9 sump should be fitted,

94

A horizontal fitment, together with downdraught carburettors, calls for some surgery to the engine cover in order to provide clearance for the air filters.

which will require slight modification to the Mk2's oil pump pick-up and oil return pipe. The Turbo unit itself is from the Mk1 because there is insufficient clearance for the Mk2 unit and its manifolding.

The transmission driveshafts need careful selection. The suggested parts are the Mk1 1300 Turbo intermediate shaft and two short X1/9 shafts. The nearside shaft will fit straight in, but the offside is short by 32mm; this is exactly the same size as the body of an X1/9 CV joint, which can be modified to suit as a spacer. It is recommended that the driveshaft couplings should be secured with grade 12.9 tensile strength bolts in place of the normal 8.8 grade. The identification is indicated on the head of the bolt. The distributor needs to be crankshaft-mounted as the area around the end of the camshaft is now occupied with the air control unit.

Cooling problems can be avoided by mounting the turbo intercooler and the engine oil cooler in the airflow from the left and right rear wing side vents.

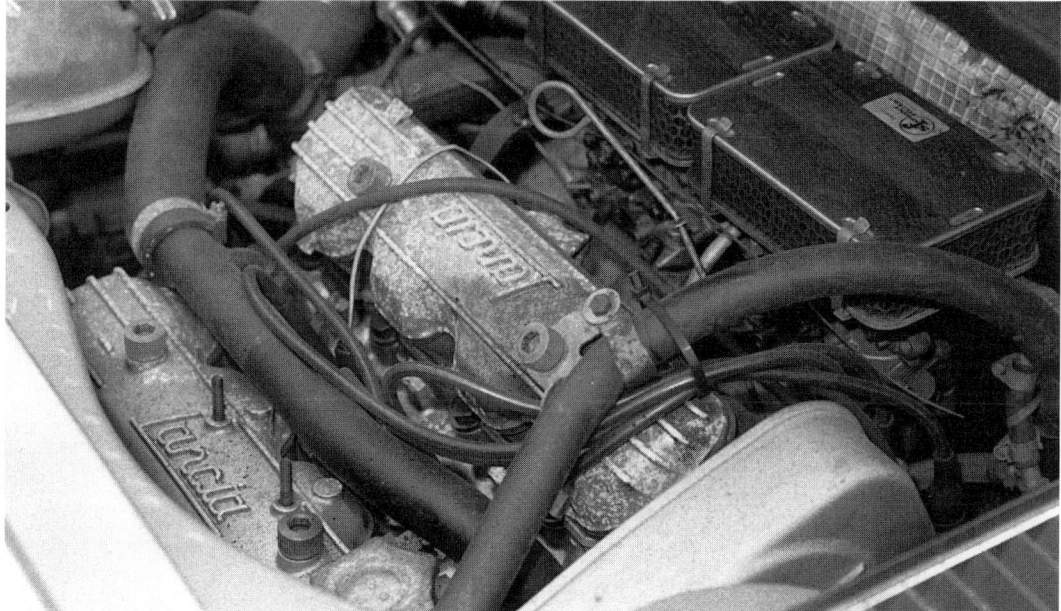

Probably the most successful arrangement is the rear inclination adopted by Geoff Oliver, of the X1/9 Centre; this installation offers better access than most.

Turbocharging is a sensible method of uprating the X1/9. The modifications can be achieved without deviating too far from the original design parameters. The external appearance of this X1/9 Turbo is completely standard, so does not betray the significant improvement in the power output.

The adoption of a 1,367cc Mk2 Uno Turbo engine with some interchange of Mk1 components offers a sensible alternative power unit. With a carefully planned layout, the X1/9 chassis requires no additional surgery.

The performance of a turbo-converted X1/9 should be similar to the Uno. Although the Uno is 40kg heavier than the sportscar, it is more efficient aerodynamically; the front of the X1/9 is quite slippery, but the airflow is interrupted by the steep rear window.

1300 to 1500
If an early 1300 is to be re-engined with the later 1500 unit, a decision will have to be made concerning the choice of gearbox. The bodyshell on the 1500 is modified to accept the longer five-speed gearbox, so a 1300 shell would have to be modified or the original four-speed unit retained.

A power unit sourced from the Fiat Strada or Lancia Delta range can be exchanged for the 1500 X1/9 engine. It should be noted that if the distributor is to be run from the crankcase drive point, a blanking cap is necessary for the end of the camshaft where the original distributor was located. This will require packing out with extra gaskets or a spacer, otherwise the cap will foul the camshaft, preventing its free rotation.

Body kits and repro panels
Jerry Brown, of Cambridgeshire-based Eurosport, produces body styling conversions for owners seeking to personalize their X1/9s. Brown suggests that the Eurosport conversions would probably reflect the modern appearance of the X1/9 if it were still in production, and some owners obviously think so because the company produces about a dozen kits a year. Providing the chosen styling kit is of good quality and it is applied with care, some conversions can look very striking.

The basic Eurosport kit costs around £600 for owner fitment. If Jerry Brown does the installation the cost is likely to be around £2,800 plus taxes. Included in this estimated cost is the price of the kit, car preparation, painting and a reasonable amount of welding. Of course, prodding around an X1/9 might reveal substantial horrors; dressing the car in glassfibre still requires metal to hang it on!

Because the X1/9 monocoque is so strong, replacing the original steel panels will not affect the structural integrity; there may also be a performance advantage in saving some body weight.

Modification of the original 1500 power unit can provide significant improvements in performance without the need for an engine transplant.

Another advantage of owning a glassfibre-panelled X1/9 is not immediately obvious: repair costs to damaged panels are going to be lower than with the standard steel parts. From an insurance point of view there is less likelihood of the car being written-off due to repair costs exceeding the car's value.

In addition to the styling kits, Eurosport provide a servicing, repair and spare parts service. They do not offer full engine tuning facilities, but they will supply the components for basic engine improvements. They recommend a sports air filter and crankcase breather; the filter improves air circulation around the carburettor, which will need to be rejetted. Jerry Brown has found that installing an electric fuel pump reduces the fuel vaporization problem.

Eurosport will also boost the braking system by installing more powerful 132 rear calipers and Tarox grooved front

The Eurosport body-styling kits offer an attractive alternative appearance for the X1/9, although opinions seem to differ as to whether or not the result is an improvement on the brilliance of Bertone's original design. Some voice the opinion that an updated X1/9 would have been similar to the Eurosport style had the car remained in production.

discs. Goodrich braided brake hoses will also provide a harder brake pedal. Other recommendations are Ansa or CSC exhaust systems and Koni suspension units.

Original panels are becoming rare, and although Fiat still list the part numbers, they probably don't exist, in particular offside rear wings. Engine lids are scarce, so if the owner could locate one of these complicated panels it would cost around £300. Eurosport offer glassfibre reproduction engine lids for about half this cost.

While the frame of the X1/9 door is quite strong, restoration is likely to require a lower panel repair section letting in. Jerry Brown reports that these are not always a good fit because the original trim line with its tapered channel is not faithfully copied.

Another area of Eurosport's X1/9 care package is their interior retrimming service. Dralon material is used for the seats and matching door side panels; the reasonably priced trim kit can be installed or offered for owner installation.

By dealing directly with the component manufacturers, Europsort are able to offer very competitive prices on X1/9 exclusive items such as brake and clutch master and clutch slave cylinders. They also provide an exchange service for the rear wishbone assemblies at about one-third the cost of the new item.

The annual X1/9 meeting at the Nurburgring is the Mecca for extremes in free expression. This British 2-litre twin-cam conversion is pulling a very novel design of trailer!

CHAPTER 9

X1/9s in competition

Under-utilized potential

In theory the Fiat X1/9 should be an excellent basis for a competition car. The mid-engined installation provides the weight distribution and excellent handling characteristics necessary for circuit racing, while for off-road applications the rear-engine, rear-wheel-drive layout offers good traction ability.

Weight is the biggest enemy of the X1/9, and in production form the car is limited when competing with other, lighter-weight rivals. However, the X1/9's structure is very strong and rigid, which makes it ideal for hanging on oversized, uprated components and coping with the competition modifications required for rallying and racing.

The X1/9 Prototipo 2000
The X1/9's first bid for competition fame began with Fiat's intention to enter the car for international rallies. The company's entry into world rallying began in 1969 with the twin-cam-powered 125 saloon, which was followed in 1970 by the 124 Spider. After initially supporting private teams, Fiat became fully committed as an official manufacturer entrant from 1971. The 124 Spider continued to be developed until 1974, and factory-prepared cars were entered for the 1975 season, at which point the 124 Spider had reached the peak of its competition development.

The high marketing profile achieved through international rally successes had done much to establish the roadgoing 124 Spider as a commercial success, especially in the lucrative US market. Fiat were now seeking to replace the 124 with another competitive car that could also be promoted commercially. The problem was that the manufacturer was suffering something of an identity crisis.

In the meantime, Lancia had been building on its competition profile with their Fulvia, a car that was being rallied in direct competition with Fiat's 124 Spider. Then in 1969 Fiat bought out Lancia, and five years later the Fulvia was replaced by the new Beta Coupe, a car that used a power unit based on the Fiat 124 Spider's engine. Simultaneously, the Ferrari-engined Stratos emerged, and this stunning car immediately dominated the competition scene, eclipsing everything else that Fiat/Lancia had prepared, so the company quickly dropped the Beta in favour of this purpose-built machine, which thereafter was used to promote Lancia as a marque, rather than establish itself as a model intended for series production.

Between 1973 and 1981, Fiat and Lancia entered rally cars in the Group 4 category, which included the Gran Turismo Speciale class, the word 'Speciale' indicating a wide range of mechanical modifications, which anticipated the later Group B regulations.

To homologate a car in Group 4, manufacturers were required to make 400 identical models within 24 months, a drop in the ocean compared with the 1993 Group A rules, which required that 5,000 cars were built in a year. There were also significant technical differences between the old Group 4 and the modern Group A regulations. For example, Group 4 offered great flexibility in the engine specification, including the fuel system, which could be injected. The suspension could also be modified, and wide wheelarches added to accommodate the oversize rims. The use of

Proof that apart from TOL 65337 there were at least four other X1/9 Prototipo cars. TOL 65336 is on the ramp, TOL 65335 is immediately behind with TOH 02940 next to it, and an unpainted car stands behind the open-top Abarth sports-racer.

plexiglass was permitted to replace the heavy standard glass windows. Manufacturers quickly took advantage of the Group 4 regulations and produced some very sophisticated cars that were to represent the peak of competition car development during the Seventies.

To keep the Fiat name in rallying, consideration was given to replacing the 124 Spider with the X1/9. After all, the new sportscar shared the same mid-engined layout as the Stratos, and therefore seemingly offered the same recipe for success.

The idea of a competition X1/9 emanated from the men of the Racing Department in the early Seventies. Fiat works driver Gino Macaluso developed the strategy for an X1/9 Abarth in association with Aurelio Lampredi, who was responsible for engine development. Testing was carried out by Giorgio Pianta.

A 1,600cc version was originally planned, using the proven

twin-cam unit fitted to the successful 124 Sport Spider, but as the Spider evolved, the development team realized that the most practical idea was to substitute the 1,800cc engine. Badged as a '2000', the X1/9 Prototipo's actual capacity was 1,840cc, derived from an 86mm bore and a 79.2mm stroke. The overbored Fiat 124 Spider engine drove through a five-speed Lancia Beta gearbox. Running with an 11.4:1 compression ratio, the unit produced between 190 and 210bhp at 7,600rpm, according to the choice of camshafts. The Abarth-designed 16-valve cylinder head, with valve angles said to be copied from the Ford DFV, was fed by two 44mm Weber downdraught carburettors.

Weighing only 750kg, the X1/9 was quicker than the 124 Spider (900kg) and the later 131 Abarth (950kg). Depending on the choice of gearing, the car could accelerate to 100km/h (62mph) in 6.2 seconds and was capable of a top

The Abarth competition department in 1974. An unpainted X1/9 Abarth is parked behind a Formula Abarth single-seater. Also to be seen are several covered sports-racers, a 124 Special, a 124 Spider, an Autobianchi A112 and a 131 saloon.

TOL 65335 displays the ventilation ducts in the bonnet that are vital for efficient airflow through the radiator. The car alongside has a different bonnet design without the ducts, and the inlet between the headlamps has been blanked-off.

speed of 200km/h.

The X1/9 made its competition debut in the 1973 Rally di Sicilia, which it failed to finish, and it also withdrew from its next rally, the Quattro Regioni. Very quickly two streams of thought were born: people who believed in the Prototipo and people who did not.

In 1974, the car was driven by Bacchelli during the Alpi Orientali rally, which it won, and it won again with Bacchelli at the wheel in the Coppa Trabucchi. At the end of that year, the Italian champion Verini, partnered by Torriani, drove the car to victory once again, this time in the Liburna rally, although Bisulli, driving a 124 Spider, had been ahead of the X1/9 and was then required by team orders to stop and let it pass.

That same year, the X1/9 was given star treatment when Clay Regazzoni, at the time a Ferrari Formula One driver, drove the car in the 1974 Giro d'Italia, his co-driver being Gino Macaluso. However, the car failed to finish. Fiat had invited Regazzoni to run the prototype as a promotion to sell the 400 road cars it was necessary to make for homologation under the Group 4 rally regulations.

It became clear that the Prototipo had high potential, but the Fiat management decided to call a halt to its competition activities: instead it was decided that Lancia, with their Stratos, had to win all the rallies.

The handful of drivers who were fortunate enough to drive the X1/9 were impressed with its performance. It was a very modern car for 1974, with its rear-mounted transverse engine and lightweight body. It also had great potential that, many believe, could have taken it to the highest levels, perhaps even greater than those achieved by the Stratos,

Detail of the rally driving lights on TOL 65337. Headlamps were fixed, not retractable as on the road cars.

The battery isolation switch and external fire extinguisher release were mounted on the engine air intake. Note the simplified pushbutton door release.

Close-up of the front suspension showing the anti-roll bar, not fitted to production cars, and the brake ducting.

Detail of the Abarth 16-valve cylinder head fitted with twin down-draught Weber 44IDF carburettors. Note the inboard distributor that runs off the exhaust camshaft.

which was harder to drive. The nimble handling character-istics were likened to the later, more powerful, but heavier Lancia 037.

For a new rally car to have been so successful in its first few outings was commendable, a circumstance that was unusual for a new car during the Seventies, when reliability was of such paramount importance in rallying. The X1/9 was inherently good, and after a few rallies it would have quickly achieved that reliability. The development potential was considerable, with opportunities for a full 2-litre engine with supercharging.

Had it not been for the fabulous Lancia Stratos, the X1/9 could, and probably would, have been a lasting success, but after its promising start it was shelved in favour of another Fiat, the 131. Through rallying, this less than attractive saloon received the exposure and publicity required to launch the car into international sales. It became a competition success, but only after the all-conquering Stratos had

A clear view of the box section that runs down the centre of the floor. Its purpose is to carry the fixed pipework for the engine coolant to the front-mounted radiator. If the internal piping corrodes on road cars, repairs to the box section are notoriously difficult to carry out. Note the front anti-roll bar.

Rear suspension detail showing the exhaust tailpipe and sump shield.

The driver's compartment was very cramped by rallying standards and bore little resemblance to the road-going car.

been prematurely retired in order to give the 131 saloon a chance.

Exactly how many X1/9 Abarths were manufactured varies according to the information source quoted. The 'Abarth man' in America, Al Cosentino, wrote in his publications that there were four cars. He claims that two were used in competition, with a third as a spare, the fourth example being a roadgoing prototype. Cosentino acquired one of the competition cars, less engine, in an unsuccessful attempt to race it at Daytona in 1977.

There are difficulties in tracing the history of the Turin Reparto Corse cars because the registration numbers were often changed. The chassis numbers are the only guarantee of accuracy as after every race Abarth kept records of them.

The huge fuel tank was mounted in the front compartment amid the ducting for the airflow into the cabin.

TOL 65336 was fitted with an eight-valve engine carrying a conventional outboard distributor. Note the remote oil filter.

The Prototipo chassis numbers run in the sequence 23001 to 23005, 23001 being the original prototype; number 23002 was destroyed. Gino Macaluso of Club Italia owns 23003, registered TOL 65336, which is complete and at the time of writing in running order. Motoring historian Graham Gauld has driven this car and believes that five chassis were constructed, three of which survive. Of the remaining two cars, 23004 and 23005, there is uncertainty as to which one still exists, but one of them is the roadgoing version.

The coachbuilders Bertone suggest that the X1/9 Prototipo 2000 was to be their basis for a high-performance road version of the standard X1/9. They recognized the potential of the production X1/9, realizing that it would benefit from the extra power and be a realistic replacement for the 124 Sport range in 1975. Naturally, Bertone had a commercial eye open and wished to court Fiat's favour, but as history relates, Fiat chose the Lancia Montecarlo route for the 124 Coupe replacement and employed Bertone's rival,

One of the modifications required to install the twin-cam power unit was the removal of the rear luggage compartment.

Unfortunately, this impressive car was not adopted as Fiat's rallying flagship, the honour falling instead to the 131 saloon. Note the increased size of air intake on the side of the rear wing.

Pininfarina, to design it. The 124 range survived beyond 1975 when the reprieved 124 Spider was produced solely for export to the United States. The Fiat X1/9 Abarth would have been a Stratos for the masses, an exciting prospect to warm the heart of the Italian sportscar enthusiast, not to mention the stage rallying and tarmac racing competitor.

So the X1/9 was not to achieve the international rallying success which it clearly deserved, neither was it to be generally recognized for its circuit abilities, although it did enjoy some success on tarmac, even though its achievements were to a considerable extent overshadowed by the larger-capacity cars which outclassed it.

Highly modified X1/9s built by Dallara have been popular with club racers. The silhouette formula allowed for extensive modifications provided the cockpit area retained its original appearance. Sophisticated Formula One-style suspension is hidden beneath the bodywork. The styling of the Dallara car is as surprising as that of the trousers worn by the pit crew and spectators!

The heart of the Dallara X1/9 was this twin-cam 1,600cc unit that was capable of developing 200bhp at an astonishing 10,000rpm. The cylinder head was Dallara's own design and featured 16 valves and mechanical fuel injection. The car's interior fittings (right) can perhaps best be described as basic.

Dallara were the first to use the X1/9 as a competition chassis in 1973, and this highly modified car produced 192bhp at 9,800rpm. 'Icsunonove' means 'X1/9'.

Dallara

While Fiat were looking at the X1/9's rallying prospects, Giampaolo Dallara was developing a racing version. The Parma-based company built its first version in 1973 to Group 5 regulations. This was a silhouette formula where unlimited mechanical modifications could be hidden under super-lightweight bodywork, these cars bearing only a vague resemblance to the production models from which they were derived.

In 1973, Dallara was a well-known racing car constructor, notably for his Formula 3 designs for the Wolf team, and he was capable of manufacturing his own alloy castings and glassfibre bodies. More than 20 years on, he continues to build racing cars, his Formula 3 chassis still being prominent, and a 16-valve Fiat Tipo-engined car having featured high up in various championships.

The Dallara X1/9 retained the original passenger compartment, but the front and rear sections of the shell were removed and replaced with subframes that reduced the body weight by 200kg. Weight-saving continued with the suspension uprights being made from magnesium alloy, and the use of single radius arms and fabricated lower suspension arms.

The power unit was fitted with an in-house-developed 16-valve cylinder head mounted on the 1,300cc block. The fuel-injected engine gave a phenomenal 192bhp at 9,700rpm.

About 30 of these cars, which included an even more powerful 1,600cc version, were manufactured by Dallara between 1974 and 1978, but although they performed well and achieved many class wins, outright victory invariably went to the bigger cars like the Porsches and BMWs.

Radbourne, prominent London Fiat dealers, were responsible for the first UK imports of X1/9s. In 1978 they acquired a Dallara rolling shell and prepared it for national circuit racing.

Radbourne Racing

Radbourne, prominent Fiat dealers in London in the Seventies, recognized that the roadgoing X1/9 was down on power and set about converting a 1300. In rejecting the popular Fiat twin-cam 1,600cc engine, which required considerable chassis alteration to accept it, they opted instead for a capacity increase on the existing engine.

They achieved a capacity of 1,625cc by having a long-stroke steel crankshaft specially manufactured by Gordon Allen. It had a 68mm stroke, 12.5mm longer than standard, together with a shorter con-rod. The bore was enlarged to 87mm. The pistons were dished to reduce the compression to a realistic level of between 9.5 and 10:1. The cylinder head remained standard, although a Stage One Abarth camshaft was fitted, and breathing was through two 40 DCNF downdraught carburettors.

A 60 per cent power improvement was estimated over the 73bhp of the standard engine, about 115bhp seeming to be realistic, with the engine spinning freely to 7,000rpm; engine torque was also increased dramatically.

The car was fitted with a modified 1,500cc engine that had Cosworth pistons and a steel crankshaft and con-rods. Carburation was via twin 45mm Webers and dry-sump lubrication was installed. The Dallara body was strengthened by an extensive tubular cage that can be seen here forming part of the roof pillars. It is said that the shell was as rigid as a contemporary Formula One car.

In 1980 the Radbourne car was rebuilt with a one-piece front end and smoother wheelarches. A 16-valve Dallara cylinder head was fitted, increasing the power output to a significant 184bhp; combined with a body weight of only 600kg, the X1/9 was now very fast indeed. In this final form the car achieved several outright race victories and won the Donington GT Championship in 1981.

Brian Cowe developed the Italian Car Services X1/9 to the absolute limit of the Italian Intermarque Championship regulations. However, unfortunately, the highly modified car, powered by a Mk1 Uno Turbo engine, was entered in only two races before it was destroyed in a fire.

The car's fully detachable front and rear body panels have been removed to reveal the huge tyres necessary to keep it on the circuit.

Radbourne also fitted the 1600 with the 8 per cent higher 128 CL 1300 final-drive, the 3.77:1 differential providing 18mph per 1,000rpm in top gear. Performance was significantly improved with the 0–60mph time down from 12.7 to a useful 9.3 seconds, and top speed was increased from 99 to 110mph.

Apparently 16 customers ordered the modified car, which cost almost twice the price of a new 1300. Radbourne raced the car in 1977 in a six-hour relay race at the Donington circuit, where it formed part of the winning handicap entry, appropriately called the Gordon Allen Crankshaft Team.

Radbourne were inspired by the 1600 X1/9's racing debut and, in 1978, obtained a rolling Dallara chassis. They installed a modified 1,500cc unit with Cosworth pistons, a steel crank and con-rods. The bore was increased to 87mm with a standard stroke. Lubrication was dry-sumped and the carburation was via twin 45mm Webers. Transmission was through a Colotti five-speed gearbox with a limited-slip

Massive Mercedes brake calipers were required to stop the ultra-light car that generated over 200bhp.

differential. Wheel sizes were 8in front and 11in rear.

The 11:1 compression engine was expected to attain 135bhp at 9,000rpm, but development difficulties with the cooling system prevented a reliable racing entry until 1979. The car was driven by the subsequent British Saloon Car Championship contender Steve Soper. Eventually, a reliable power output of 143bhp at 8,250rpm was achieved, maximum revs being set at an astonishing 10,000rpm.

By 1980, the car was setting lap records and achieved three outright victories and reliable power had been increased to 162bhp. As a result of fitting a 16-valve Dallara head, Radbourne were able to gain another 22bhp, maximum power now being up to 184bhp, and with only 600kg of body weight the car had become very fast indeed.

Radbourne also prepared a production-based X1/9 for racing driver Costas Los; they were able to extract 98bhp from the 1500 and run it reliably to 7,500rpm. Apart from the exhaust system, the power unit was standard, the extra 13bhp over the original output being achieved by blueprinting. Radbourne then sold their Dallara to Costas Los for him to continue his eventful career and they prepared a new car for Steve Soper to run in 1982. Subsequently, the ex-Costas Los Dallara went to Sweden, and is believed to have been used there in rallycross events.

Italian Intermarque Championship
The British Racing and Sports Car Club's Italian Intermarque Championship was created in 1985, based on a series of 10 races visiting most of the UK circuits. With several levels of specification, this popular championship is open to all production-based Italian sports and saloon cars.

A number of X1/9s have raced in the Intermarque classes, including 1300 production, modified 1600 and 2000 twin-cams, and an exotic 1300 turbo.

Club racer Bruce Kennedy has been running a 1974 left-hand-drive 1300 model, which is one of the oldest X1/9s in the UK. Kennedy originally purchased his X1/9 in 1979 and drove it in Holland as an everyday car. Realizing that the X1/9 was a good basis for a club racer, he converted it to run in the BRSCC Production Sports Championship when, under Uniroyal sponsorship, he became Class C Champion

Probably the fastest X1/9 to have competed in recent UK club racing championships, this car was proof enough of the competition capabilities of the design for modern sportscar racing.

Intense wheel-changing activity in a grassy paddock for the Radbourne X1/9, which was driven by Steve Soper, one of Britain's top Touring Car drivers in the Nineties.

Once run regularly in rallycross events, this 1,600cc twin-cam-powered car was later raced on British club circuits.

Several companies adopted the X1/9 as a basis for supplying body styling kits, this being an example of the Faran Eliminator that appeared briefly at Mallory Park in 1989. This particular car had a Lancia 2-litre twin-cam engine.

Ashley Bristow ran his Guy Croft-tuned 1300 X1/9 in club racing before moving on to rallying, when he found the car ideal for forest stage events. Here he is cornering hard at Snetterton while being pursued by a 500bhp De Tomaso Mangusta.

in 1984. Bruce moved on to the Italian Intermarque Challenge in 1986 and had several successful seasons, becoming Class F Champion in 1992. He reported that the set-up and running costs of the X1/9 were relatively low.

Brian Cowe, of Darlington-based Italian Car Services, also chose the excellent handling characteristics of the mid-engined X1/9 for a sports-racing car. This car was radically modified, making full use of the silhouette regulations adopted for modified cars in the championship.

Cowe's car was 18in wider than the production model and was fitted with massive 10in front and 14in rear wheels, shod with Formula 3000 racing tyres. Suspension was by fully adjustable Leda units and the Mercedes brake calipers acted on Fiat Croma Turbo discs.

The engine was basically a fuel-injected Mk1 1300 Uno Turbo unit fitted with a Holbay camshaft and an F1 Micro Dynamics fifth injector. The turbo chosen was a Garrett T3, and the intercooler was from a Ford Cosworth RS1600. Rear-engined turbo installations require a considerable redesign of the cooling system to cope with the extremely

Bristow's X1/9 showing the effectiveness of the mid-engined layout on the 'rough'.

high temperatures generated. Cowe overcame these problems by installing Formula 1-style radiators immediately in front of the rear wheels.

Power figures in excess of 200bhp were recorded before the car began to spin the rollers on the rolling road! After initial testing this monster was just becoming reliable and competitive when unfortunately it was destroyed in a garage fire.

National rallying

Ashley Bristow has covered most types of events in his X1/9 and has proved how versatile and competitive the car can be.

His car was fully modified with a Guy Croft-tuned engine and made its first competition appearance in the Italian Intermarque Championship. He won his class in 1989 and achieved several high overall race positions.

Bristow decided to move on to national rallying, reshelling the car in preparation. Particular attention was paid to

strengthening and lightening, a glassfibre bonnet, bootlid and front wings being fitted, the doors stripped and Perspex windows installed.

Major overheating problems were overcome by getting as much air as possible through the front-mounted radiator, this being achieved initially by improving the air exit, hence the huge vents in the bonnet.

The brakes and suspension were uprated and some home-made improvements included front and rear brake servos sourced from BMW. A fly-off handbrake and bias pedal box were also chosen, and the 6-gallon fuel tank was located in the front compartment to help place extra weight over the front wheels.

After a shake-down rallycross event at Lydden Hill, where Bristow finished a creditable second overall, he launched himself into rally events and like others who have seen the sportscar's potential, has been proving that the X1/9 can be a very competitive vehicle.

A study in styles. Compared with the standard car, the X1/9 Prototipo 2000 looks very dramatic, its huge wheels and extended wheelarches presenting a most determined appearance.

Fiat X1/9 technical specifications

Fiat X1/9 1300

Engine 128.AS
Chassis 128.AS

Cubic capacity	1,290cc
Bore	86mm
Stroke	55.5mm
Compression ratio	9.2:1
Power	73bhp at 6,000rpm
Torque	10.3kgm (74.5lb.ft) at 3,400rpm
Oil pressure	50/71psi at 85deg
Valve diameter	inlet 36mm, exhaust 31mm
Valve lift	9.75mm
Valve timing	12'52'52'12'
Carburettor	Weber 32 DMTR34

Transmission

Clutch		181.5mm (7.1in)
Gearbox ratios	1st	3.583:1
	2nd	2.235:1
	3rd	1.454:1
	4th	0.959:1
	Rev	3.714:1
Final-drive		4.077:1 (53/13)

Brakes

Front discs	227mm (8.9in)
Rear discs	227mm (8.9in)

Steering

Rack and pinion

Camber angle	laden	– 1deg + or – 20min
	unladen	0deg to – 1deg
Castor angle		7deg + or – 30min
Wheel alignment	laden	3mm + or – 1mm toe-in
	unladen	2–6mm toe-in

Front suspension

Spring length	170mm (6.69in) at 210kg + or – 10kg (441/485lb)

Rear suspension

Camber angle	laden	– 2deg + or – 20min
	unladen	– 1deg 10min to – 2deg 10min
Wheel alignment		4–6mm toe-in
Spring length		200mm (7.87in) at 250kg + or – 10kg (540/584lb)

Electrical system

Static ignition timing	5deg BTDC
Spark plugs	Champion N9Y
Plug gap	0.6/0.7mm (.024/.027in)

Distributor	Marelli S135B or Ducellier
Contact breaker gap	Marelli: 0.37/0.43mm (.015/.017in)
	Ducellier: 0.35/0.50mm (.014/.019in)
Dwell angle	55deg + or – 3deg
Alternator	Bosch G1-14v-33A27
Starter motor	Fiat E84-0.8/12

Capacities

Engine oil	5 litres (8.8 pints)
Transmission	3.15 litres (5.5 pints)
Cooling system	11 litres (19.4 pints)
Fuel tank	48 litres (10.6 gallons)
Tyre size	145 x 13
Pressures	Front 1.8bar (26psi)
	Rear 2.0bar (28psi)

Dimensions

Length	3,830mm (12ft 7in)
Width	1,570mm (5ft 2in)
Height	1,170mm (3ft 10in)
Track	front 1,335mm (4ft 4½in)
	rear 1,343mm (4ft 5in)
Wheelbase	2,202mm (7ft 3in)
Weight	880kg (17.3cwt)

Torque settings

	kgm	lb.ft
Cylinder head nuts	9.5	61.5
Big-end nuts	5	36
Main bearing nuts	8	58
Flywheel bolts	8.5	61.5
Clutch to flywheel bolts	1.5	10.8
Crownwheel bolts	7	51
Road wheel nuts	7	51
Steering wheel nut	5	36

Fiat X1/9 1500

Engine 138.BS
Chassis 128.AS1

Cubic capacity	1,498cc
Bore	86.4mm
Stroke	63.9mm
Compression ratio	9.2:1
Power	85bhp at 6,000rpm
Torque	12kgm (87lb.ft) at 3,200rpm
Oil pressure	50/71psi at 85deg
Valve diameter inlet	36mm, exhaust 33mm
Valve lift	inlet 9.85mm, exhaust 9.90mm
Valve timing	24'68'68'24'
Carburettor	Weber 34 DATR7/250

Transmission

Clutch	190mm (7.5in)	
Gearbox ratios	1st	3.583:1
	2nd	2.235:1
	3rd	1.454:1
	4th	1.042:1
	5th	0.863:1
	Rev	3.714:1
Final-drive	4.077:1 (53/13)	

Brakes

Front discs	227mm (8.9in)
Rear discs	227mm (8.9in)

Steering

Rack and pinion

Camber angle	laden – 0deg 30min/ – 1deg 30min
	unladen 0deg/ – 1deg
Castor angle	7deg + or – 30min
Wheel alignment	laden 1–5mm
	unladen 2–6mm toe-in

Front suspension

Spring length	170mm (6.69in) at 215kg + or – 10kg (441/485lb)

Rear suspension

Camber	laden – 2 degrees + or – 20 mins unladen – 1 degree 10 mins to – 2 degrees 10 mins
Wheel alignment	4–6mm toe-in
Spring length	200mm (7.87in) at 250kg + or – 10kg (540/584lb)

Electrical system

Static ignition timing	5deg BTDC
Spark plugs	Champion RN7Y
Plug gap	0.7/0.8mm (.028/.031in)
Distributor	Marelli S135LX or Ducellier 525IA
Contact breaker gap	Marelli: 0.37/0.43mm (.015/.017in) Ducellier: 0.35/0.50mm (.014/.019in)
Dwell angle	55deg + or – 3deg
Alternator	Bosch G1–14v–33A27
Starter motor	Fiat E84-0.8/12

Capacities

Engine oil	5 litres (8.8 pints)
Transmission	3.15 litres (5.5 pints)
Cooling system	11 litres (19.4 pints)
Fuel tank	48 litres (10.6 gallons)
Tyre size	145 x 13
Pressures	front 1.8bar (26psi) rear 2.0bar (28psi)

Dimensions

Length	3,830mm (12ft 7in)
Width	1,570mm (5ft 2in)
Height	1,170mm (3ft 10in)
Track	front 1,335mm (4ft 5 ½ in) rear 1,343mm (4ft 5in)
Wheelbase	2,202mm (7ft 3in)
Weight	880kg (17.3cwt)

Torque settings

	kgm	lb.ft
Cylinder head nuts	9.5	61.5
Big-end nuts	5	36
Main bearing nuts	8	58
Flywheel bolts	8.5	61.5
Clutch to flywheel bolts	1.5	10.8
Crownwheel bolts	7	51
Road wheel nuts	7	51
Steering wheel nut	5	36

Fiat X1/9 Abarth

Engine	rear transverse, 4 cylinders in line.
Capacity	1,840cc
Bore	86mm
Stroke	79.2mm
Compression ratio	11.4:1
Valve gear	twin-cam, 16 valves
Carburettors	2 x Weber 44 IDF
Maximum power	200bhp at 7,600rpm
Transmission	5-speed gearbox with limited-slip differential
Steering	rack and pinion

Dimensions

Length	3,810mm
Width	1,690mm
Tyres front	8in x 13in
rear	235/550/13in
Weight	750kg

APPENDIX B

Fiat family technical specifications and performance transplants

128 Saloon	1100	1300	Special	Rally
Capacity (cc)	1,116	1,290	1,290	1,290
Bore (mm)	80	86	86	86
Stroke (mm)	55.5	55.5	55.5	55.5
Compression	9.2:1	9.2:1	8.9:1	8.9:1
Bhp/rpm	55 @ 6,000	60 @ 6,000	60 @ 6,000	67 @ 6,400
Torque lb.ft/rpm	58.5 @ 3,000	73.7 @ 3,900	66.5 @ 3,000	65 @ 4,000
Valves inlet	36	36	36	36
exhaust	30.5	30.5	30.5	31
Valve lift	9.1	9.75	9.75	9.75
Cam timing	12/52 52/12	20/44 60/4	20/44 60/4	24/68 64/28
Carburettor	32ICEV	32ICEV18	32ICEV18	32DMTR20
Gear ratios	1.042 1.454 2.235 3.583	1.042 1.454 2.235 3.583	1.042 1.454 2.235 3.583	1.037 1.454 2.235 3.583
Final-drive	3.77:1	3.77:1	3.77:1	4.077:1
(Estate)	4.077:1	4.077:1		

128	Coupe/3P	Coupe	Coupe	3P
Capacity (cc)	1,116	1,290	1,116	1,290
Bore (mm)	80	86	80	86
Stroke (mm)	55.5	55.5	55.5	55.5
Compression	8.8:1	8.9:1	8.8:1	9.2:1
Bhp/rpm	64 @ 6,000	75 @ 6,600	64 @ 6,600	73 @ 6,000
Torque lb.ft rpm	61 @ 4,400	68 @ 3,600	61 @ 6,000	74 @ 3,900
Valves inlet	36	36	36	36
exhaust	30.5	30.5	30.5	30.5
Valve lift	9.75	9.75	9.75	9.75
Cam timing	12/52 52/12	24/68 68/24	12/52 52/12	12/52 52/12
Carburettor	32DMTR20	32DMTR20	32DMTR20	32DMTR32
Gear ratios	1.042 1.454 2.235 3.583	1.042 1.454 2.235 3.583	1.042 1.454 2.235 3.583	1.042 1.454 2.235 3.583
Final-drive	4.077:1	4.077:1	4.077:1	4.077:1

Standard camshafts at a glance

Year	Model	cc	Timing	Valve lift (mm)
1977	X1/9	1,290	12/52/52/12	9.75
1980	X1/9	1,498	24/68/68/24	9.85 (in), 9.90 (ex)
1973	128 Coupe	1,100	12/52/52/12	9.75
1973	128 Rally	1,290	24/68/64/28	9.75
1977	128 3P	1,290	12/52/52/12	9.75
1977	128 Saloon	1,290	20/44/60/4	9.75
1977	128 Saloon	1,100	12/52/52/12	9.1

Performance camshafts (Kent)

Application	Power band (rpm)	Timing	Lift (mm)
Fast road	2,000-6,000	35/67/67/35	10.54/10.33
Rally	2,500-6,000	52/76/76/52	10.82/10.61
Race	3,000-7,000	52/82/82/52	11.20/10.99

Comparative engine specifications for modified engine transplant purposes

Uno Turbo	Mk1	Mk2
Type	146A2	146A8
Capacity (cc)	1,301	1,372
Bore (mm)	80.5	80.5
Stroke (mm)	63.9	67.4
C/R	7.7:1	7.8:1
Bhp/rpm	105 @ 5,750	116 @ 6,000
Torque lb.ft/rpm	108 @ 3,200	119 @ 3,500
Valves inlet	43.5	36
exhaust	33	33
Lift	8	8.8/9.5
Cam timing	0/40 30/10	14/44 36/6
Gear ratios	0.863	0.875
	1.043	1.029
	1.469	1.440
	2.235	2.267
	4.091	3.909
Final-drive	3.588:1	3.353:1

Lancia Beta twin-cam power units

These specifications are typical, but depend on the year and model of the donor vehicle.

Lancia Beta	1600	2000	Montecarlo
Type	828A	828B	134AS
Bhp/rpm	100 @ 5,800	115 @ 5,500	120 @ 6,000
Torque kgm/rpm	13.1 @ 3,000	17.9 @ 3,000	16.8 @ 3,400

Clubs, suppliers and services

Clubs

Fiat X1/9 Owners Club
M Weaver
12 Strathmore Avenue
Hull HU6 7HJ
Great Britain

Fiat X1/9 Register
N Thornhill
284a Wickham Road
Croydon CRO 9UT
Great Britain

Fiat Motor Club (GB)
L Collyer
Barnside
Glastonbury BA6 8DB
Great Britain

Fiat Club Australia
C Roach
PO Box 1119
Canberra City ACT 2601
Australia

Fiat Club Belgio
P Bacquert
PO Box 10
B-2018 Antwerpen 11
Belgium

Fiat Club Finland
A Pohjolan-Pirhonen
Velskolan Kattano
02980 Espoo
Finland

Amateurs de Fiat d'epoque
P Lorrhioir
80 Quai Michelet
92532 Levallois Perret
France

Fiat X1/9 5-Speed Club-Suedwest
H Jordan
Neuhaeuseler Strasse 52
6670 St Inghert-Hassel
Germany

Fiat X1/9 Club Deutschland
H Mikosch
Forst Strasse 99
4100 Duisburg 1
Germany

X1/9 Club Baden
D Schaller
Postfach 6932
7500 Karlsruhe 1
Germany

Fiat X1/9 Club Nederland
H Martens
Keimate 5
6663 KB Lent
Holland

Registro Fiat Italiano
A Amadelli
via Bruno Buozzi 6
10121 Torino
Italy

Fiat Owners Club New Zealand
D Matthews
PO Box 11217
Wellington
New Zealand

Fiat Lancia Unlimited
PO Box 193
Shillington
PA 19607
USA

Fiat Rear Engine Cars Club
M Weiss
PO Box 682
Sun Valley
CA 91353
USA

General servicing and restoration

The X1/9 Centre
Unit 1, Rectory Road
Southall
Middlesex UB2 4DY
Tel: 081 574 2437

The X1/9 Man
3 Station Garage Mews
Estreham Road
Streatham
London SW16 5NT
Tel: 081 677 7799

Rossi Engineering
85 Vicarage Road
Sunbury on Thames
Middlesex TW16 7QD
Tel: 0932 786819

Alternative Autos
Staley House
38a Church Street
Heckmondwike
West Yorkshire WF16 0AX
Tel: 0924 409403

Middle Barton Garage
53–55 North Street
Middle Barton
Oxfordshire OX7 7BH
Tel: 0869 40289

The Old Forge Garage
The Green
Ealing
London W5 5DA
Tel: 081 567 4010

Italian Car Services
35 Girton Walk
Darlington
County Durham DL1 2YF
Tel: 0325 469790

Car sales and servicing

DTR European Sports Cars
16F Crown Yard
off Amyand Park Road
St Margarets
Twickenham
Middlesex
Tel: 081 891 4043

Road and race engine building

Guy Croft Tuning
Unit 2, Keel Court
Enterprise Close
Medway City Estate
Rochester
Kent ME2 4LY
Tel: 0634 290451

General servicing, restoration and body styling

Eurosport
Unit 6b
London Road Industrial Estate
Sawston
Cambridge CB2 4EF
Tel: 0223 835848

General servicing and race preparation

Barry Waterhouse Engineering
The London Car Centre
Pelier Street
London SE17 3JG
Tel: 071 703 2225

Spares and panels

Spitfire UK
Unit 11a, Branson House
West Avenue
Wigston
Leicester
Tel: 0533 812129

Interparts of London
207 Hanworth Road
Hounslow
Middlesex TW3 3UA
Tel: 081 570 8646

Car transportation and storage

Edmund Rudler
PO Box 11
Swindon
Wiltshire SN4 7SY
Tel: 0793 853159

APPENDIX D

Performance figures

The following figures are reproduced with the kind permission of *Autocar* and *Motor*, now a combined publication, whose meticulous performance-measuring procedures over the years have ensured their reputation for unsurpassed reliability and authenticity.

	X1/9 1300 4-speed	X1/9 1300 5-speed	X1/9 1500 4-speed	X1/9 1500 5-speed
Mean maximum speed (mph)	99	104	110	107.7
Acceleration (sec)				
0–30mph	3.6	3.7	3.1	3.1
0–40mph	5.9	5.8	5.0	4.7
0–50mph	8.7	8.4	7.8	7.1
0–60mph	12.7	11.8	10.8	9.9
0–70mph	17.3	15.6	14.4	13.2
0–80mph	25.5	21.8	18.1	18.3
0–90mph	41.6	31.5	25.6	25.4
0–100mph	–	–	42.8	–
Standing ¼mile (sec)	18.8	18.5	17.0	17.2
Top gear (sec)				
20–40mph	11.7	10.8	11.2	10.3
30–50mph	11.4	10.0	10.0	10.0
40–60mph	11.7	9.6	10.0	10.6
50–70mph	13.5	11.0	10.5	11.0
60–80mph	16.5	12.8	12.4	12.8
70–90mph	23.2	16.9	15.7	16.6
Overall fuel consumption (mpg)	30.7	26.1	26.8	28.0
Typical fuel consumption (mpg)	34	31	29	34
Kerb weight (lb)	2,016	1,848	2,010	2,016
Original test published	*Autocar* 19.3.77	*Motor* 25.5.74	*Autocar* 13.3.85	*Motor* 27.1.79